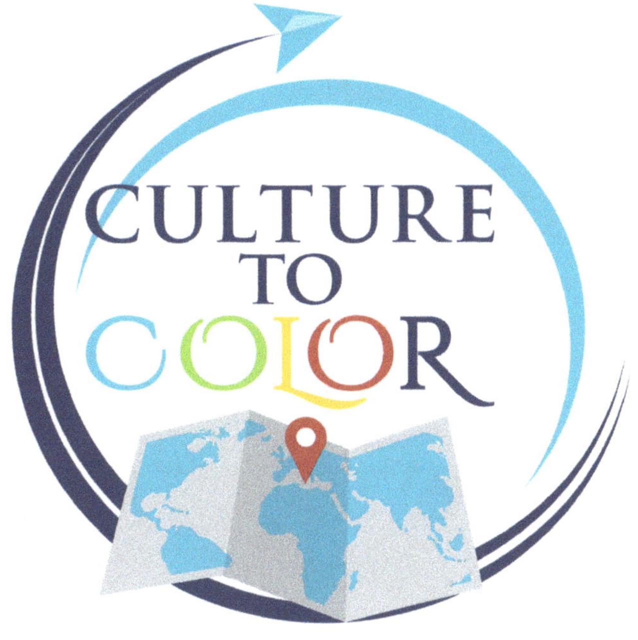

For the artist in you - coloring adventures around the globe. No suitcase necessary!

Explore the Sights Of

MOUNT DORA
FLORIDA

A Coloring Book by Bibi LeBlanc

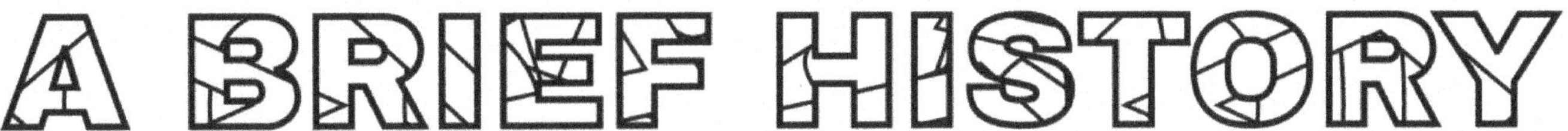
A BRIEF HISTORY

Ranking among Choice Awards' "Top 50 Best Small Towns in America," Mount Dora is a favorite vacation destination for Floridians and out-of-state tourists alike. The town's charming appeal extends well beyond its picturesque lakefront and canopy-oak tree-lined streets. This hospitable town offers a beautiful Historic Downtown with eclectic restaurants, antiques markets, boutiques, historic inns and Bed &Breakfasts, and no fewer than 30 festivals each year.

Historians believe that Mount Dora's resource-rich land was once home to the Timucua Native Americans, who fished, hunted, and farmed native vegetables. Fragments of pottery and of shell or stone ornaments date back hundreds of years. The Timucua's disappearance in the 17th century is attributed to diseases brought into Florida by Europeans.

In 1874, the first American settlers arrived. In 1882, the first school was established. Ross C. Tremain established the first post office in 1883. The town was first named Royellou after Tremain's three children, Roy, Ella and Louis, and was later renamed Mount Dora. Located on a plateau a mere 185 feet above sea level, Mount Dora was named to spotlight its rare geographical attribute in the otherwise flat state of Florida.

Flourishing flora and fauna, a warm climate, and a beautiful lakeside location quickly made Mount Dora a popular winter destination for hunters, fishermen and boaters. This spurred development of the two-story Alexander House in 1883, which has hosted such dignitaries as President Calvin Coolidge, President Dwight Eisenhower and Henry Ford. Renamed Lakeside Inn, the hotel is among the last of the grand Victorian era hotels, and the oldest continuously operating hotel in the state.

In 1886, Mount Dora had 174 residents, printed its first newspaper, The Mount Dora Voice. In 1887, the railroad brought industry and transformed the town into a small city. J.P. Donnelly built the Queen Anne-style Donnelly House in 1893 as a gift to his wife. In 1910, the town was incorporated, and Donnelly became the first mayor of Mount Dora.

Other notable historic buildings are Mount Zion Primitive Baptist Church, built by African-American homesteaders on the southern edge of town, and the William Watt House – now the Grandview Bed and Breakfast Inn – which irrigated local orange groves with its windmill. The Mount Dora Yacht Club, established in 1913, served as a USO for servicemen during World War II, and still holds an annual sailing regatta.

At the turn of the century, a clay bicycle path was constructed to connect Eustis and Mount Dora with Altamonte Springs and Sanford. The very first fire station and jail have since been transformed into Mount Dora's History Museum, which is home, among many other things, to the first ballot box and early land-promotion materials.

Despite economic challenges of the 1920s, Mount Dora's residents wanted a central location for the arts, and united to raise enough funds to build the Mount Dora Community Building. The Mediterranean-style structure opened with 800 seats — one for every town resident at that time — and continues to host concerts, private movie screenings, weddings, corporate events and theatrical performances.

A number of parks were created in Mount Dora so residents and visitors can enjoy the towns beautiful native ecosystem. The 8-acre Palm Island Nature Preserve offers hiking trails under towering cypress trees and a boardwalk where you can see nesting ospreys, herons and egrets.

In 1981, many of the city's buildings were temporarily painted pink for the film Honky Tonk Freeway. Since then, the Starry Night House, painted after Vincent van Gogh's famous masterpiece, has become a new monument to artistic freedom.

Today, Mount Dora with its charming Downtown and many festivals, including the Craft Fair, Renninger's Antique Extravaganza, the Mount Dora Music Festival, the annual Christmas-Lighting Festival, and the Plant & Garden Fair, among others, draws thousands of visitors annually. Mount Dora is truly "Someplace Special"!

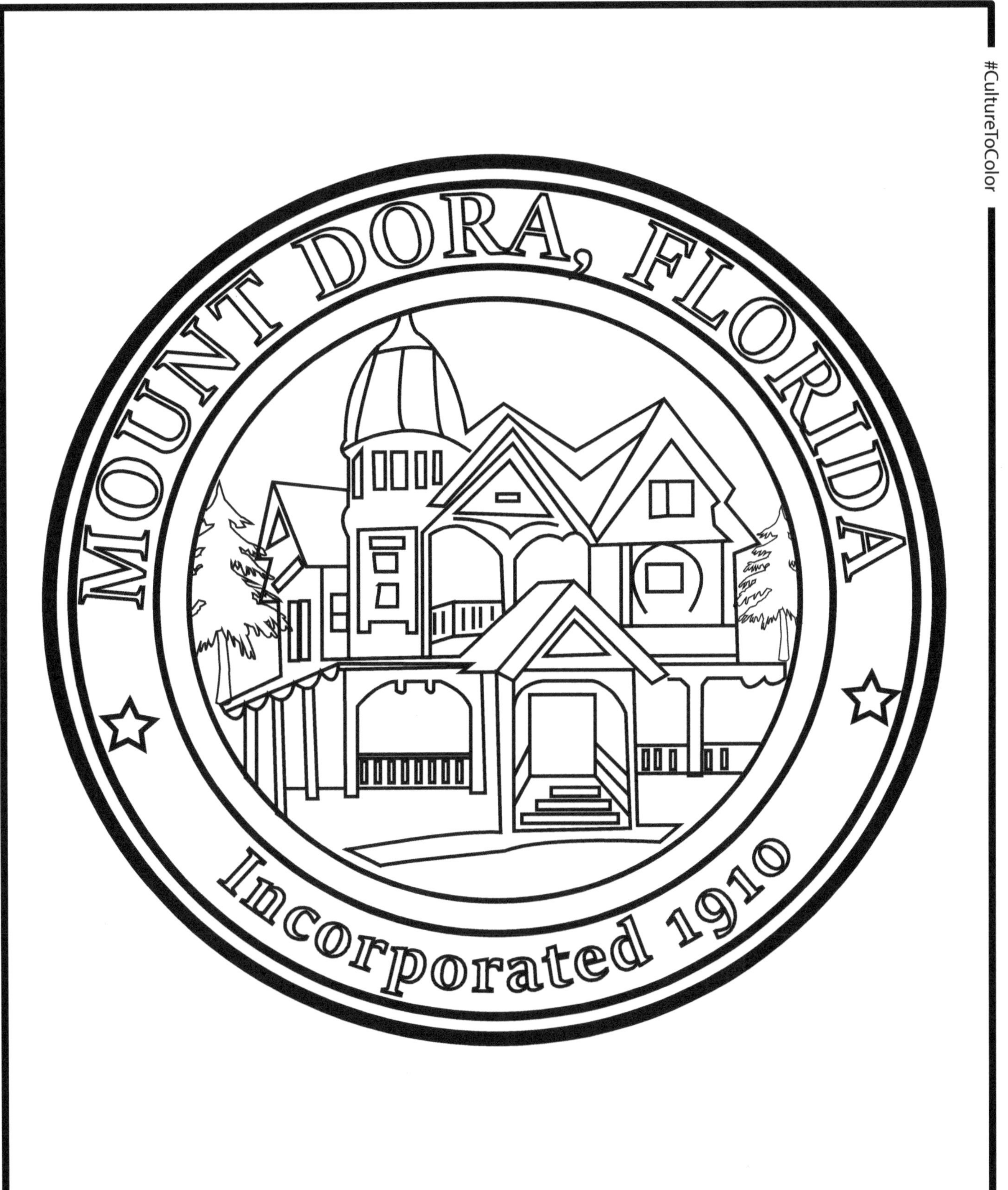

Seal of Mount Dora

Mount Dora truly is "Someplace Special," with a charming, one-hundred-plus-year-old historic village in the heart of Central Florida on the shores of beautiful Lake Dora. Whether you're traveling for fun or business, or looking for a special place to live, come visit the tree-shaded streets and swap stories with the local merchants. You haven't experienced the real Florida until you've visited Mount Dora!

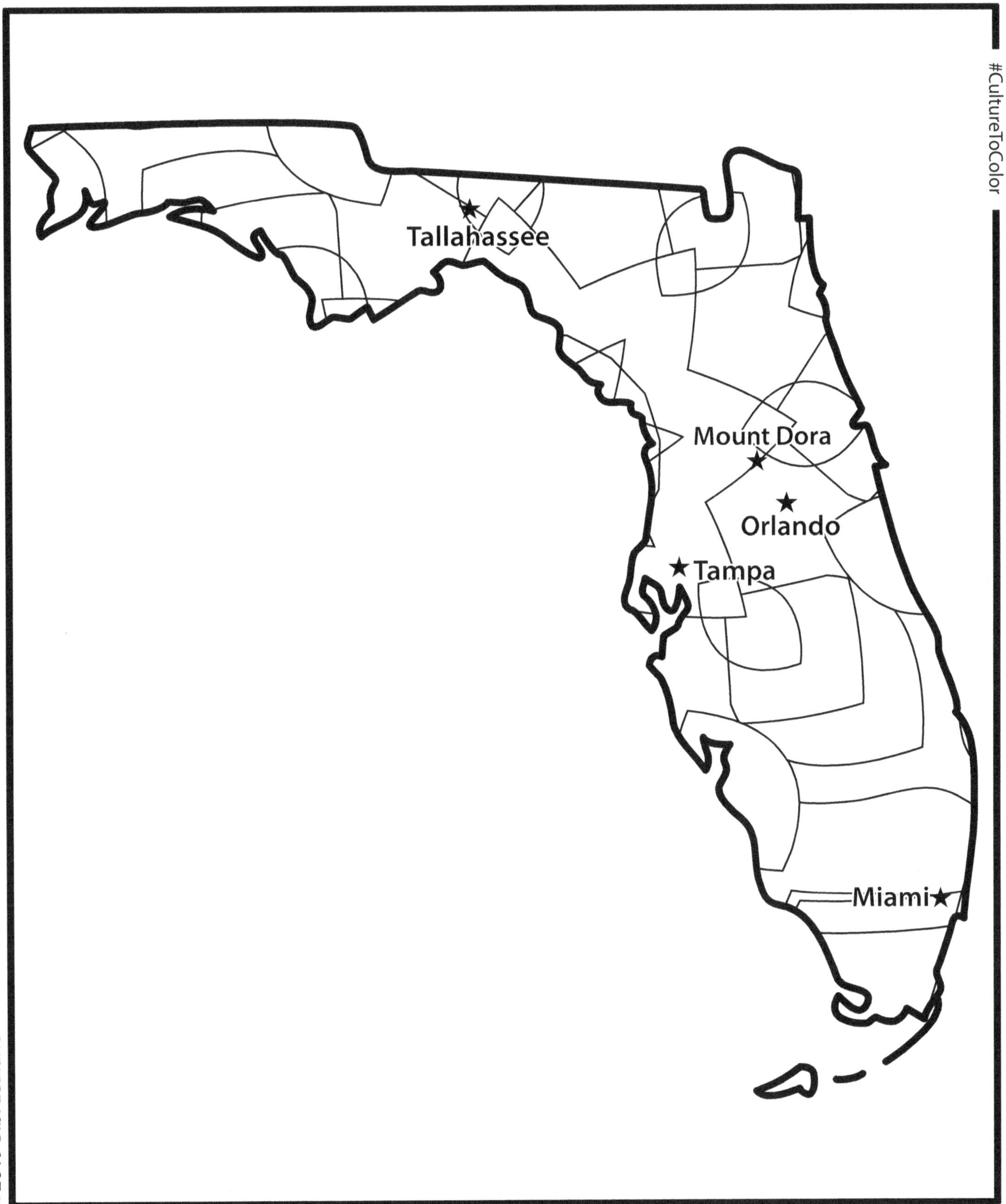

Florida

Florida (Spanish for "land of flowers") is a reflection of influences and multiple inheritances: African, European, indigenous and Latino heritages can be found in the architecture and cuisine. Florida has attracted many writers, such as Marjorie Kinnan Rawlings, Ernest Hemingway and Tennessee Williams, and continues to attract celebrities and athletes. It is internationally known for surfing, golf, tennis, auto racing and water sports.

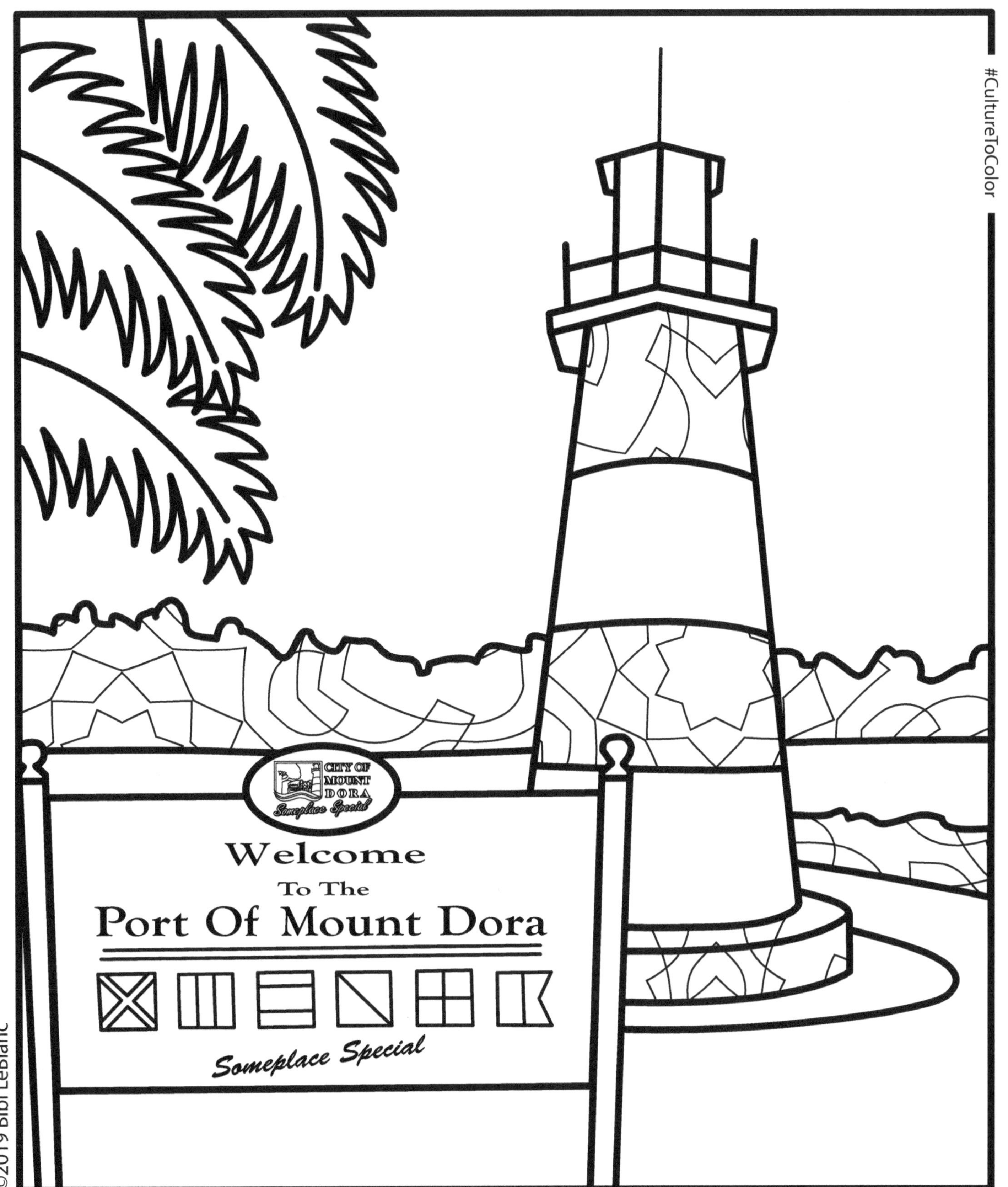

Lighthouse at Grantham Point Park

Located across from Gilbert Park on Lake Dora, Grantham Point Park was created from road rubble and fill to create one of Mount Dora's famous landmarks — the 35- foot lighthouse. Built to represent the "Port of Mount Dora," the lighthouse appears on many symbols and is considered by many "Mount Dora's Favorite Spot." Its 750-watt photocell powers a blue pulsation, sending out aguiding light to all boaters navigating Lake Dora after dusk. The Mount Dora Light is the only inland freshwater lighthouse in Florida.

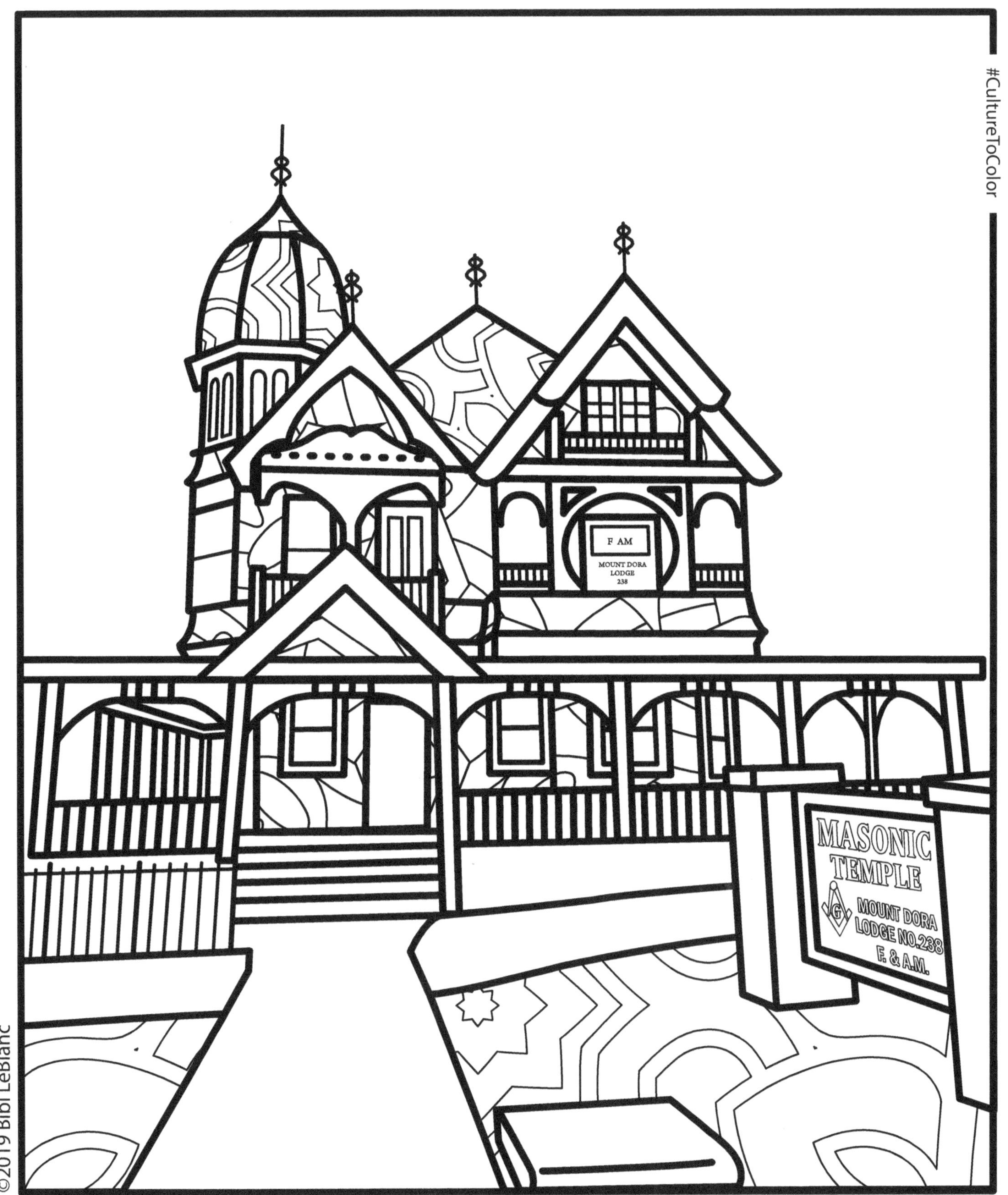

Donnelly House

John P. Donnelly came to Mount Dora in 1879. In 1881, he married Annie McDonald Stone. Successful in real estate and business ventures, Donnelly built this imposing Queen Anne-style house in 1893 as a gift to his wife. He was elected the city's first mayor in 1910. The Donnelly House, now owned by Mount Dora Lodge No. 238. F&AM, was listed on the National Register of Historic Places in April 4, 1975.

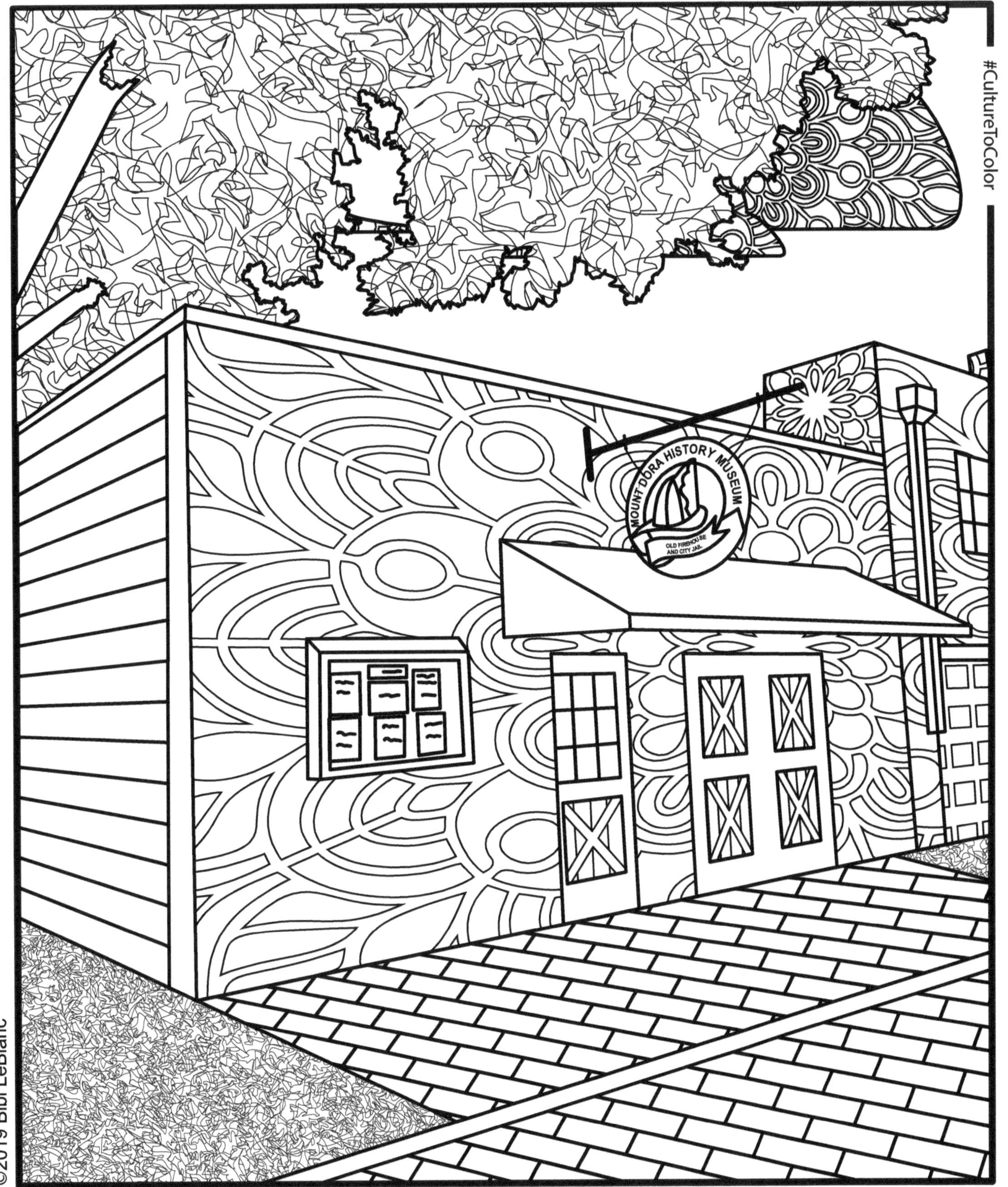

Museum of History

The Mount Dora History Museum is the signature project of the Mount Dora Historical Society. The museum is housed in the city's first fire station and jail, which was opened in 1923. The exhibits highlight activities in Mount Dora from the 1880s to the 1950s. The Historical Society also offers speakers and events throughout the year to highlight the history of the area and enhance people's awareness of the region.

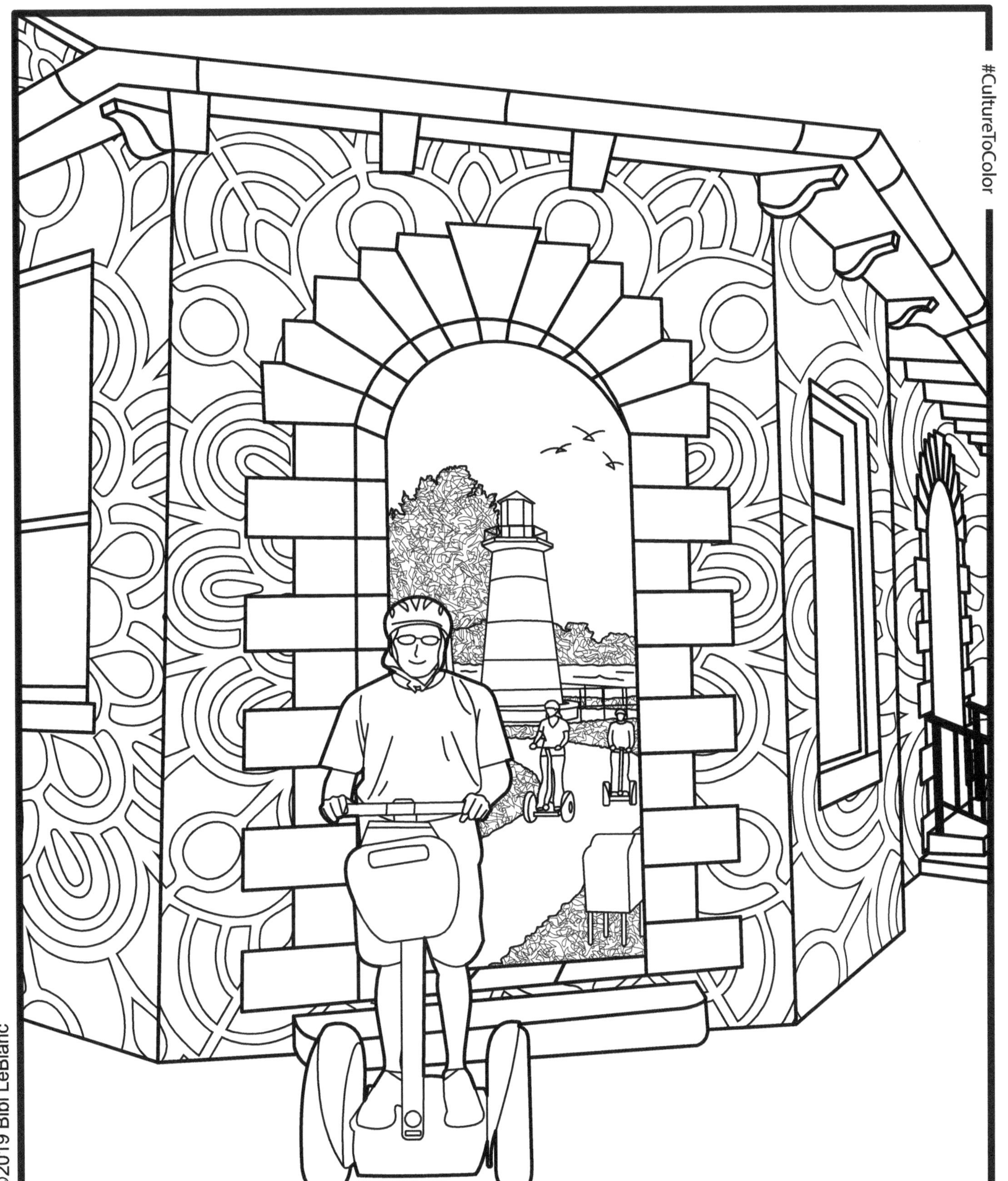

Segway of Central Florida

Enjoy a unique Segway PT City Tour of Historic Mount Dora. Travel alongside the town's expansive waterfront and city marina, to the Lighthouse and over to Palm Island Park and through historic neighborhoods. Enjoy the breathtaking view across Lake Dora before riding back to home base in the Post Office, one of the only buildings that still exhibits its original façade, on Alexander Street.

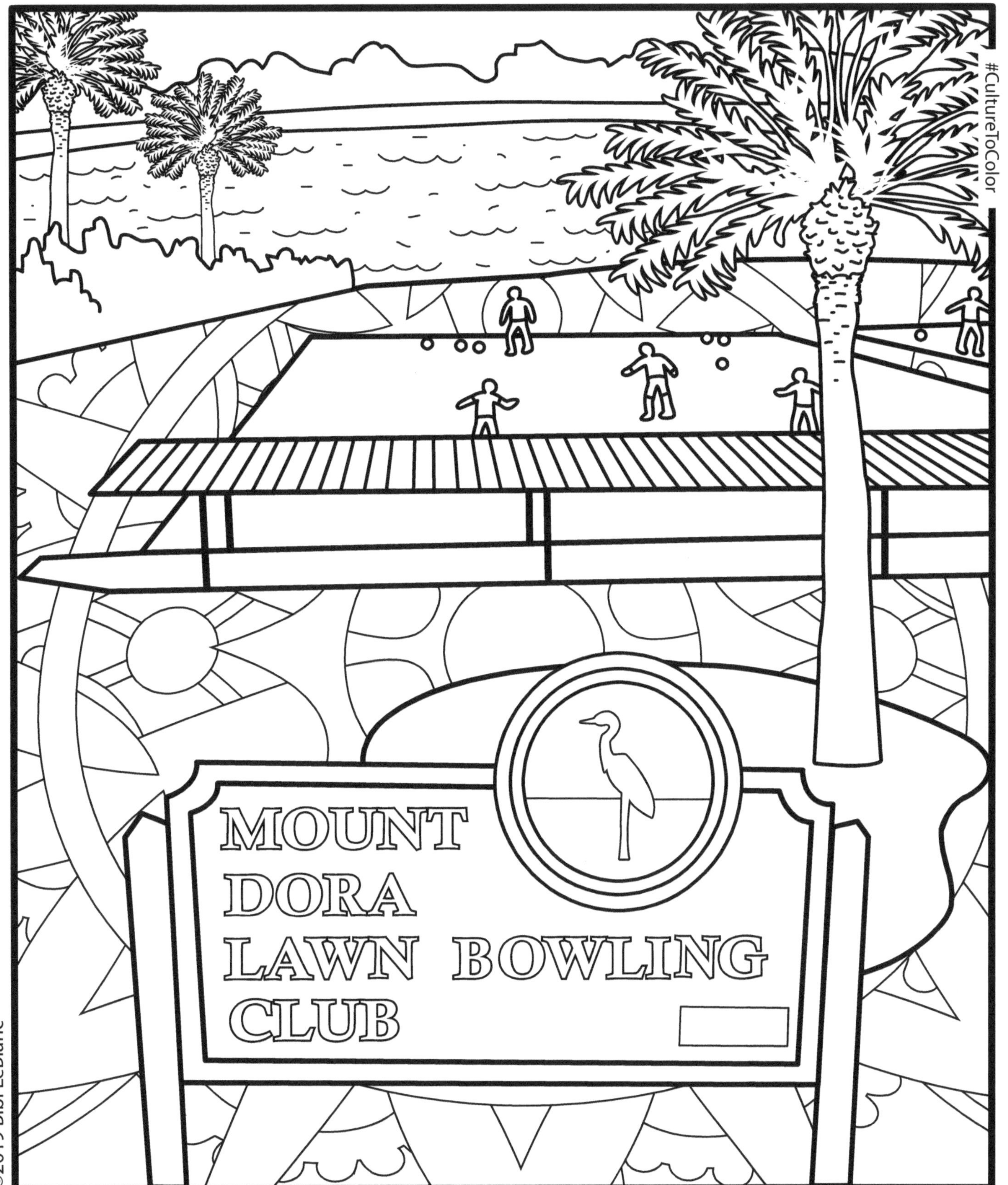

Lawn Bowling Club

The Mount Dora Lawn Bowling Club is one of the largest Bowls USA-affiliated clubs in the U.S. and offers great exercise, lots of social activities and the friendliest atmosphere in town. Come visit to play, relax, and make new friends. "Happiness is Lawn Bowling" is the club's motto!

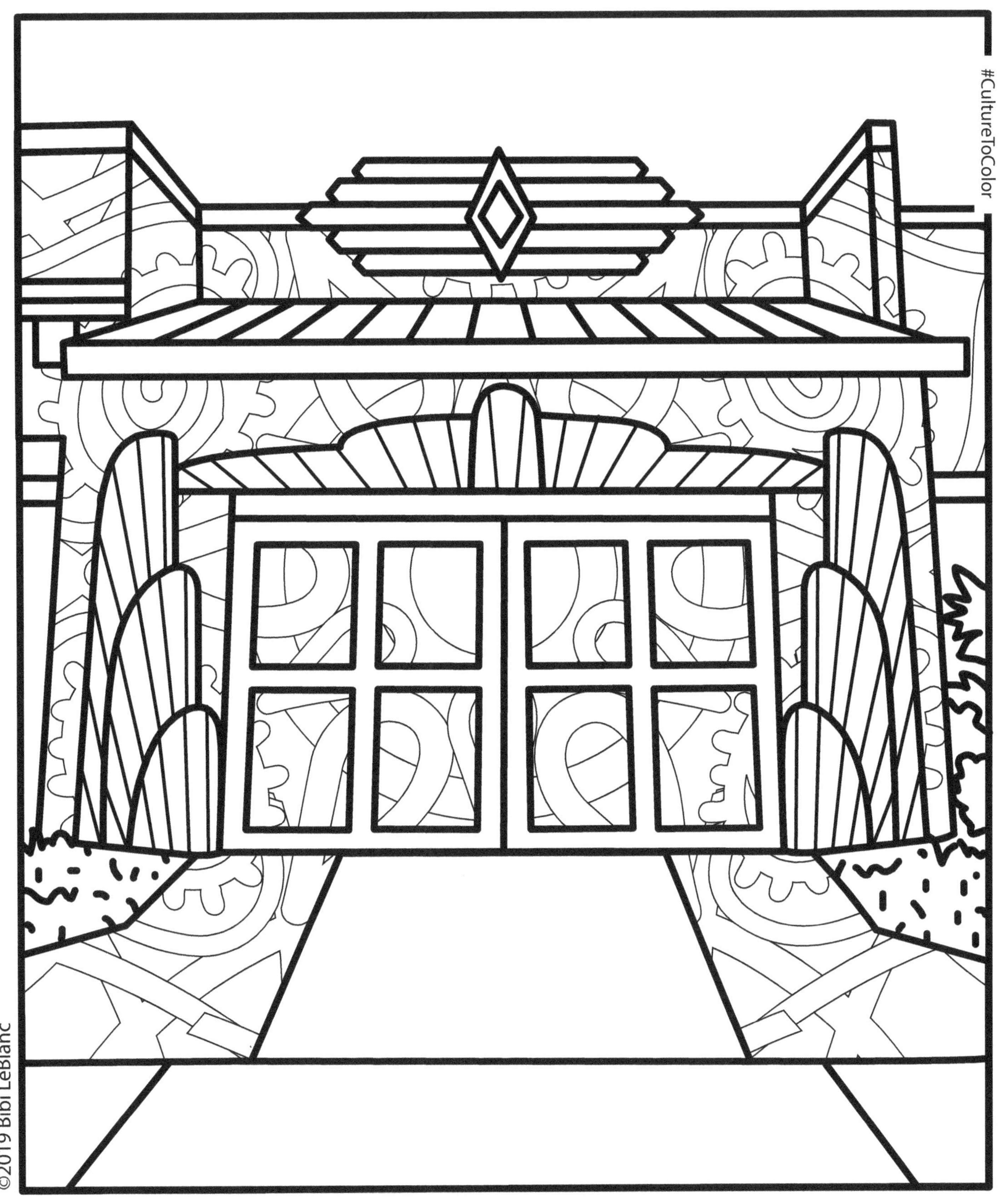

Sonnentag Theatre at the IceHouse

In 1948, residents of Mount Dora met to discuss forming a little theater. A former ice plant with perfect acoustics was located. The IceHouse Players opened to a full house February 7, 1949. In 1957, on land donated by the municipality, the current 270-seat facility at 1100 N. Unser Street was built. It opened in 1958 with "The Solid Gold Cadillac". The Sonnentag Theatre at the IceHouse is dedicated to benefiting all of Central Florida.

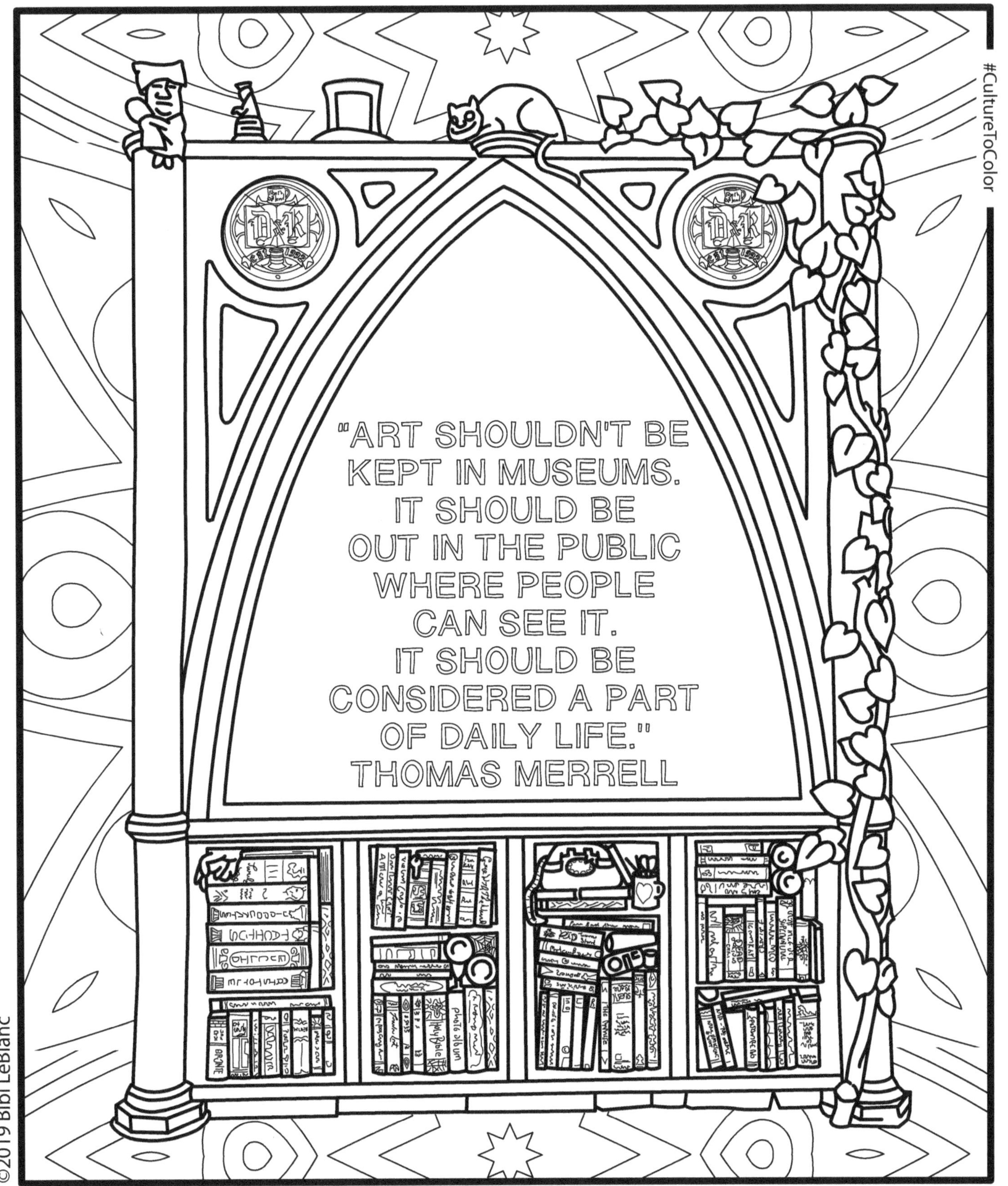

Dickens-Reed Wall

This beautiful relief wall was commissioned by Barry and Ruth Blake, then the owners of the local bookstore and coffee shop Dickens-Reed Books & Gifts. Sculptor Thomas Merrell created a unique piece of art: bas-relief scenes of bookshelves that have become part of the building, and local lore, depicting many favorite local hangouts and characters.

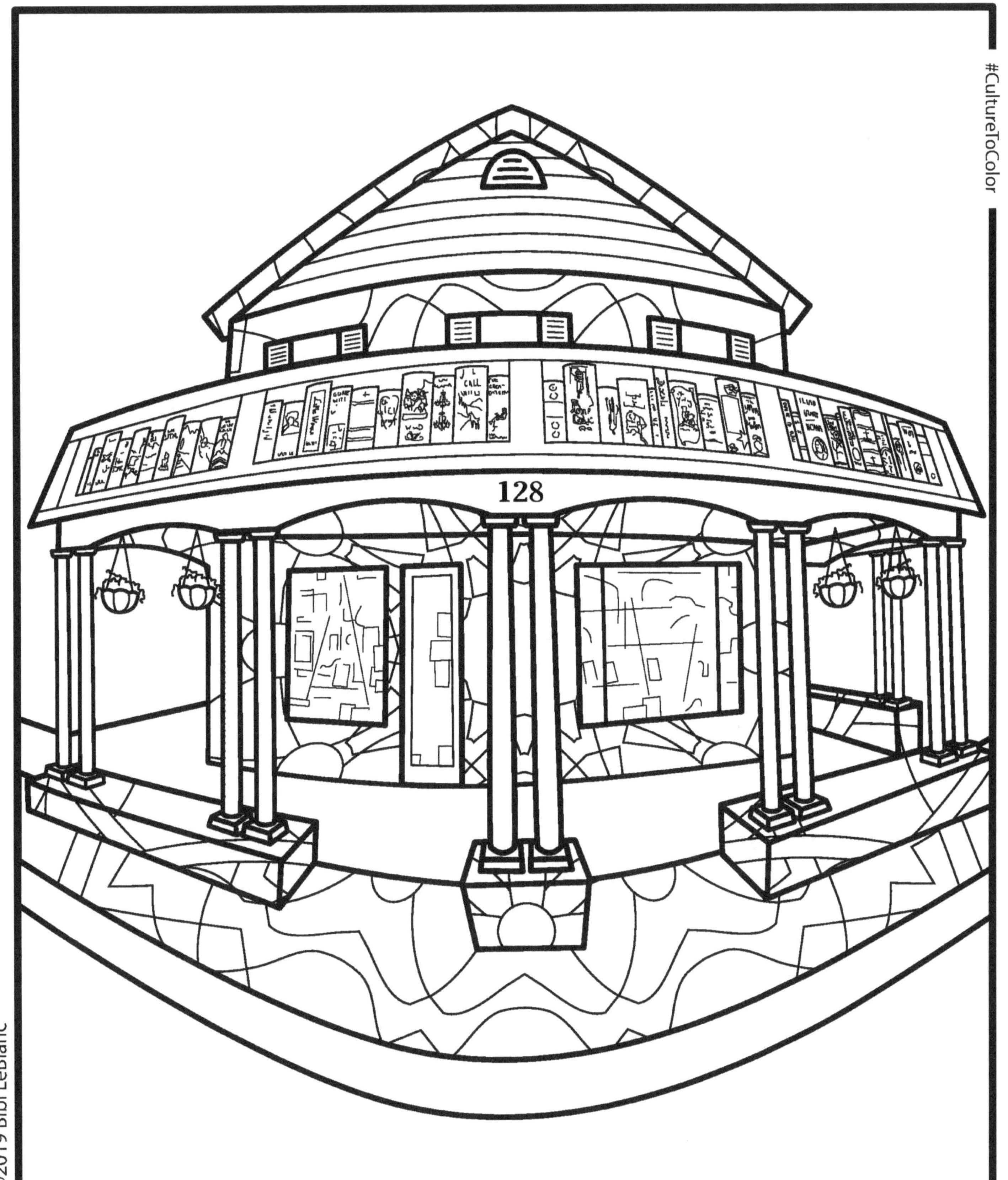

Barrel of Books and Games

A Barrel of Fun on Fourth Avenue, Mount Dora's Downtown bookstore reads like a pop-up book of surprises. Barrel of Books and Games sells a mix of new and used books in all genres and for all ages and hosts a variety of events and book-signings. The beautiful mural has been created by local artist Amy Sellers.

Mount Dora Brewing and Rocking Rabbit Brewery

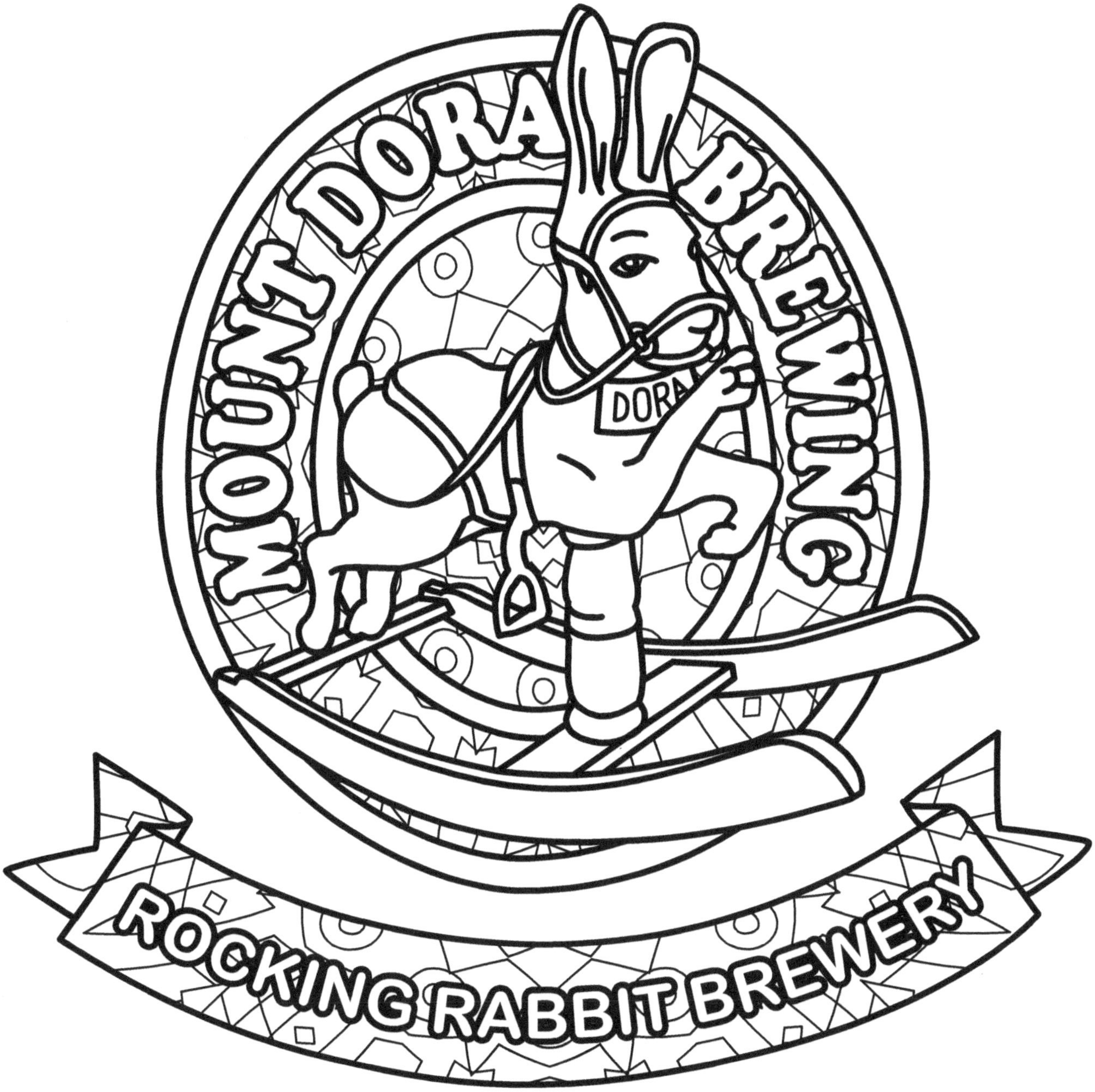

Florida's only mountain-brewed beer, brewed on-site with organic ingredients! Join your friends and neighbors in the funky Rocking Rabbit Tap Room for live music or open-mic night and acoustic jam sessions, and enjoy the dining room or outdoor Beer Garden to dine and relax.

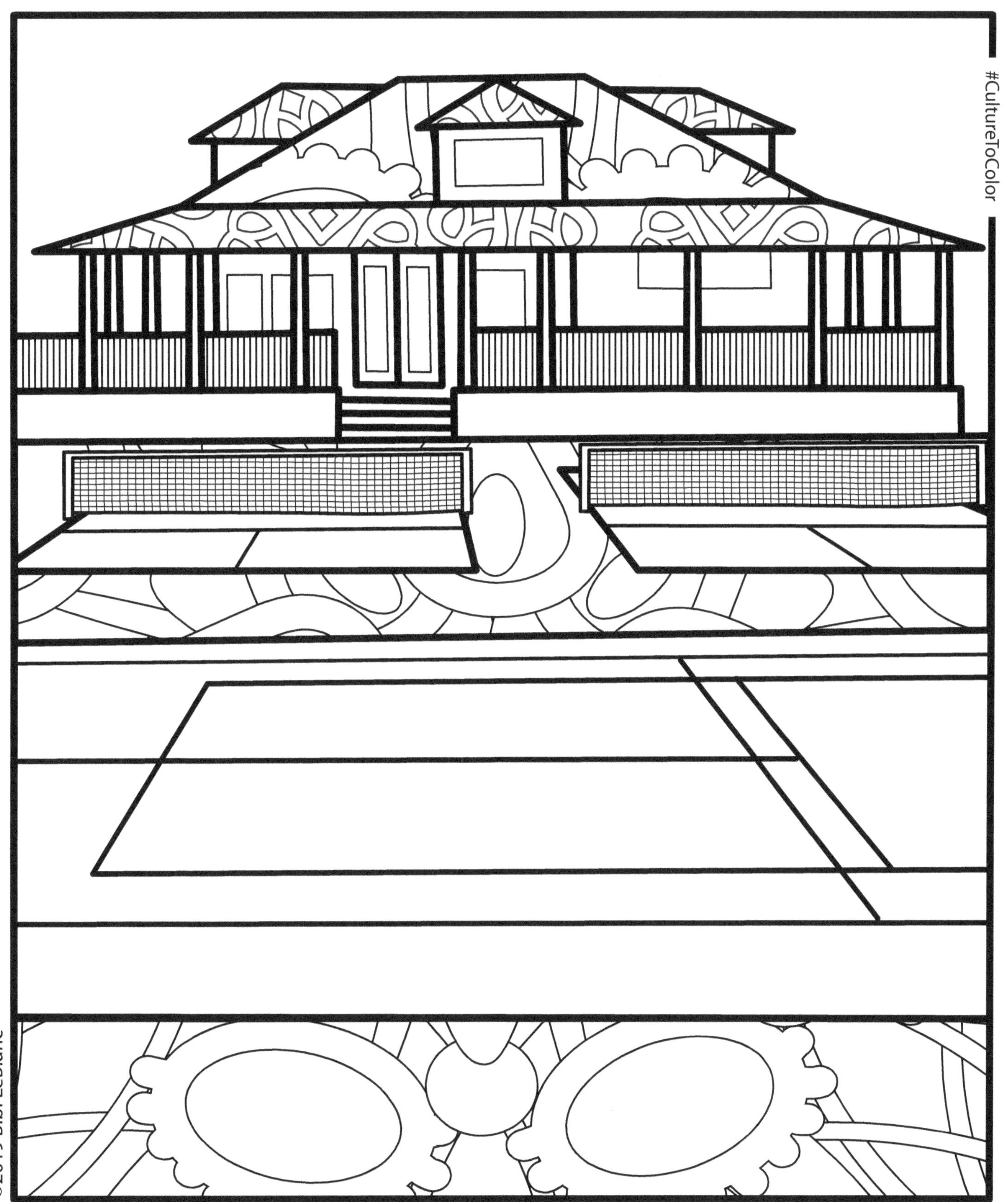

Donnelly Park

Donnelly Park is the location of the Christmas Tree-Lighting, an annual event that draws thousands of people to witness the lighting of more than 2 million Christmas lights. Many other special events and community activities are held in the park throughout the year. It is also home to the Mount Dora Pickleball Society.

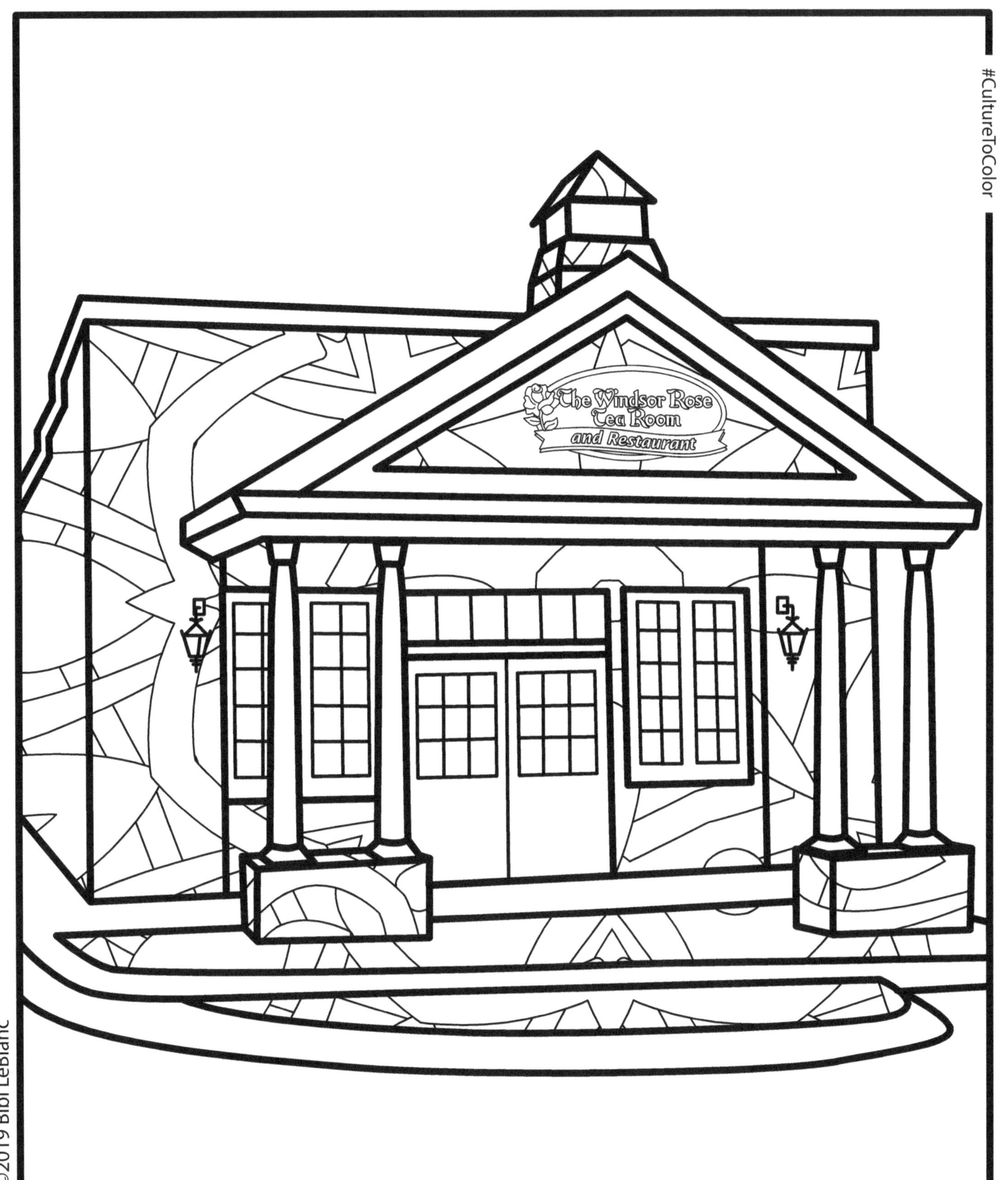

The Windsor Rose Restaurant and British Tea Room

In Downtown Mount Dora, The Windsor Rose Restaurant and British Tea Room transports you to Britain with their various teas and dishes, from pastries to meals named after towns in England. The Windsor is steeped in royal history, which makes it a destination for those who are interested in dining among the Kings and Queens.

Pipe Band and Scottish Highland Festival

The City of Mount Dora Pipe Band is a nonprofit organization with members from the local area. The City has embraced the Scottish/Celtic culture with several events, including their now annual Scottish Highland Festival, Burns Night, Kirkings and golf tournament. Mount Dora is a sister city with the city of Forres, Scotland and actively supports the cultural exchange between the two cities and their citizens.

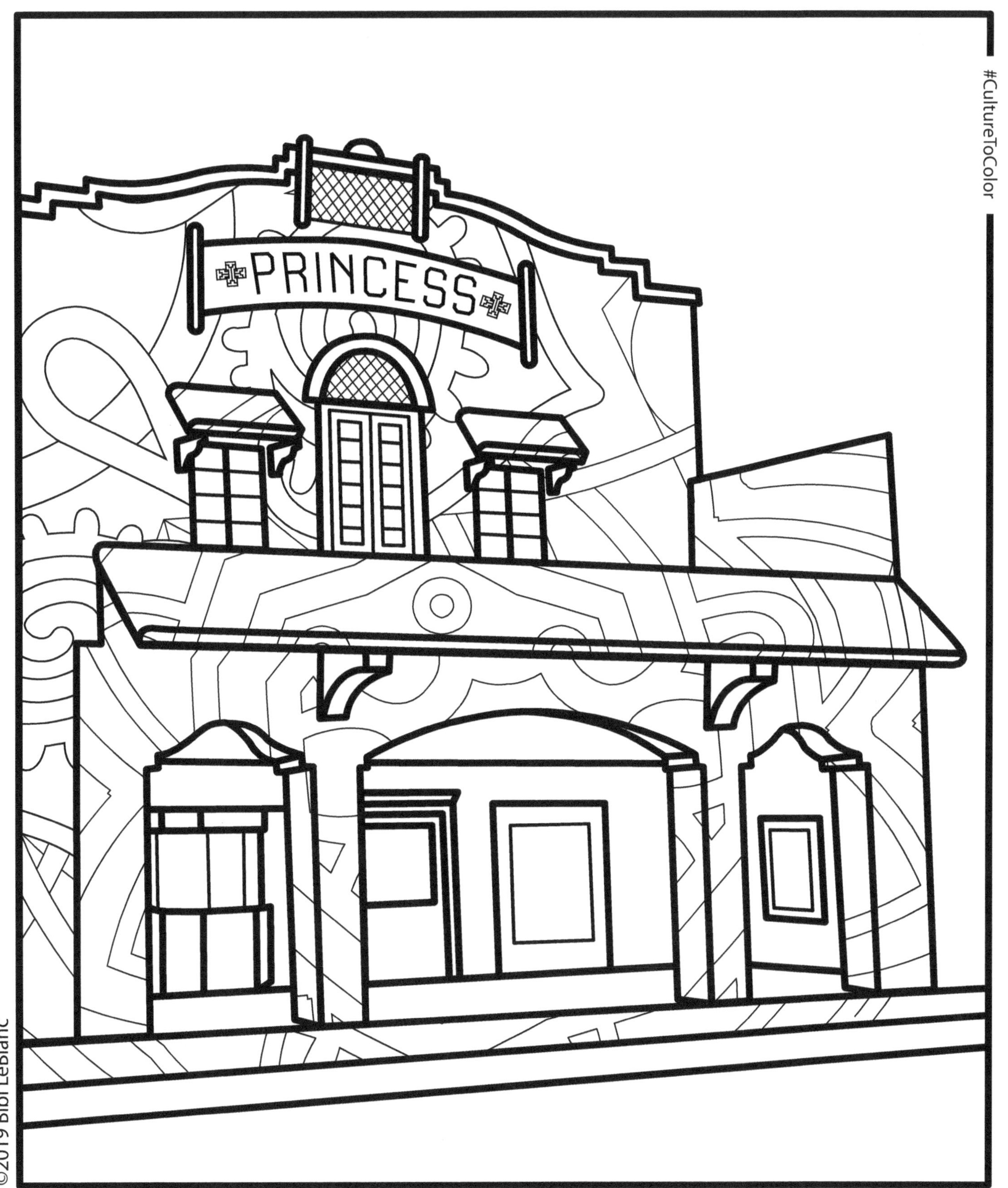

Princess Theater

Built by David S. Simpson in 1922 as a movie theater, the Princess Theatre began showing "talkies" in 1947. It served that purpose until 1972. In 1965, the Spanish front gave way to a mansard roof in keeping with the "New England" theme of Downtown. Since then, it has served many purposes, including as a nightclub.

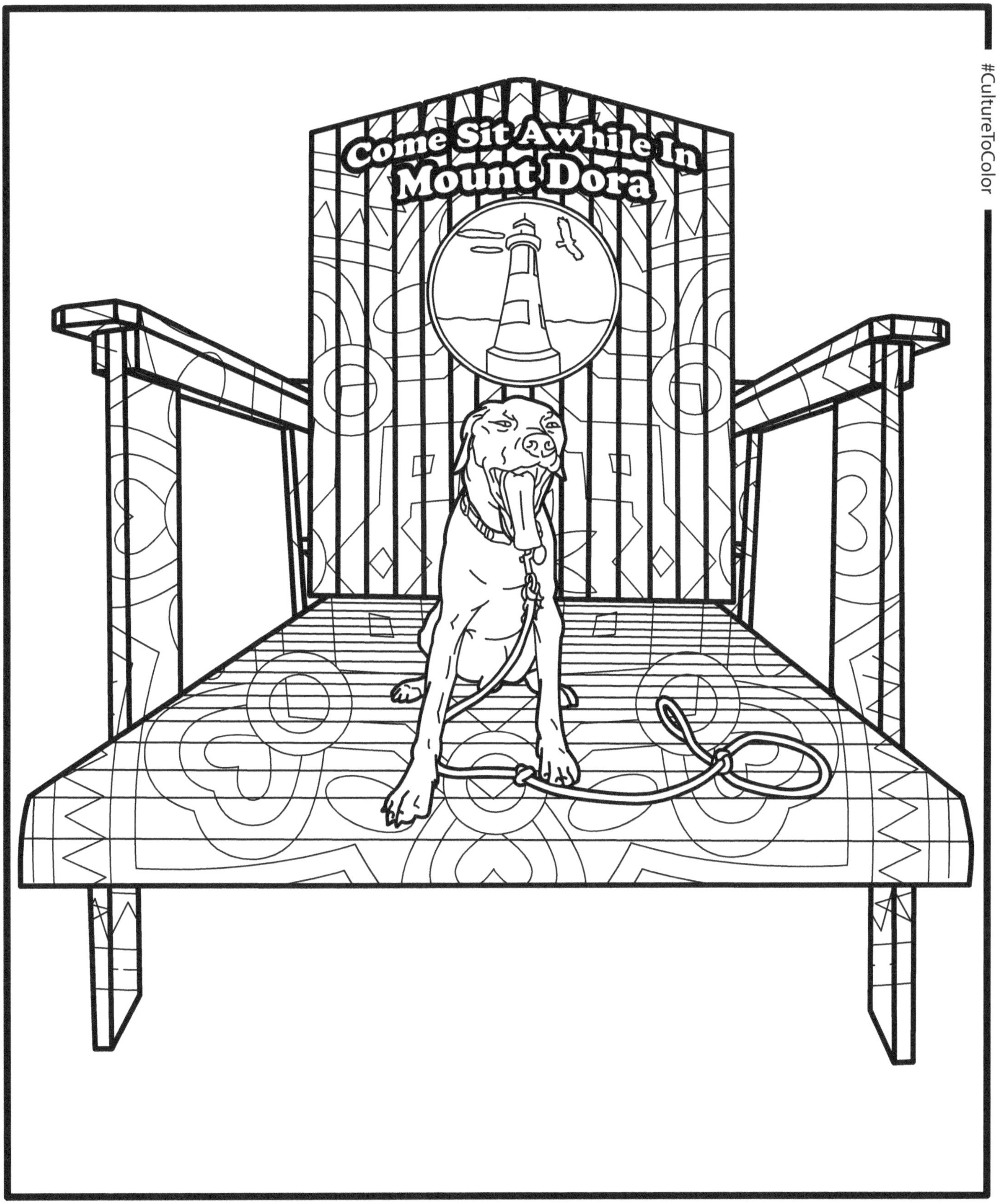

Come Sit Awhile In
Mount Dora

Come Sit a While - Grantham Point Park

Mount Dora's parks offer something for everyone. Enjoy the beautiful views, bring out the kids to the playground at Gilbert Park, or walk the boardwalk and enjoy the fishing pier at Palm Island Park. You can even rent facilities for special events like birthday parties and weddings. And the big chair at Grantham Point Park seems to invite climbers and sitters for novelty photos.

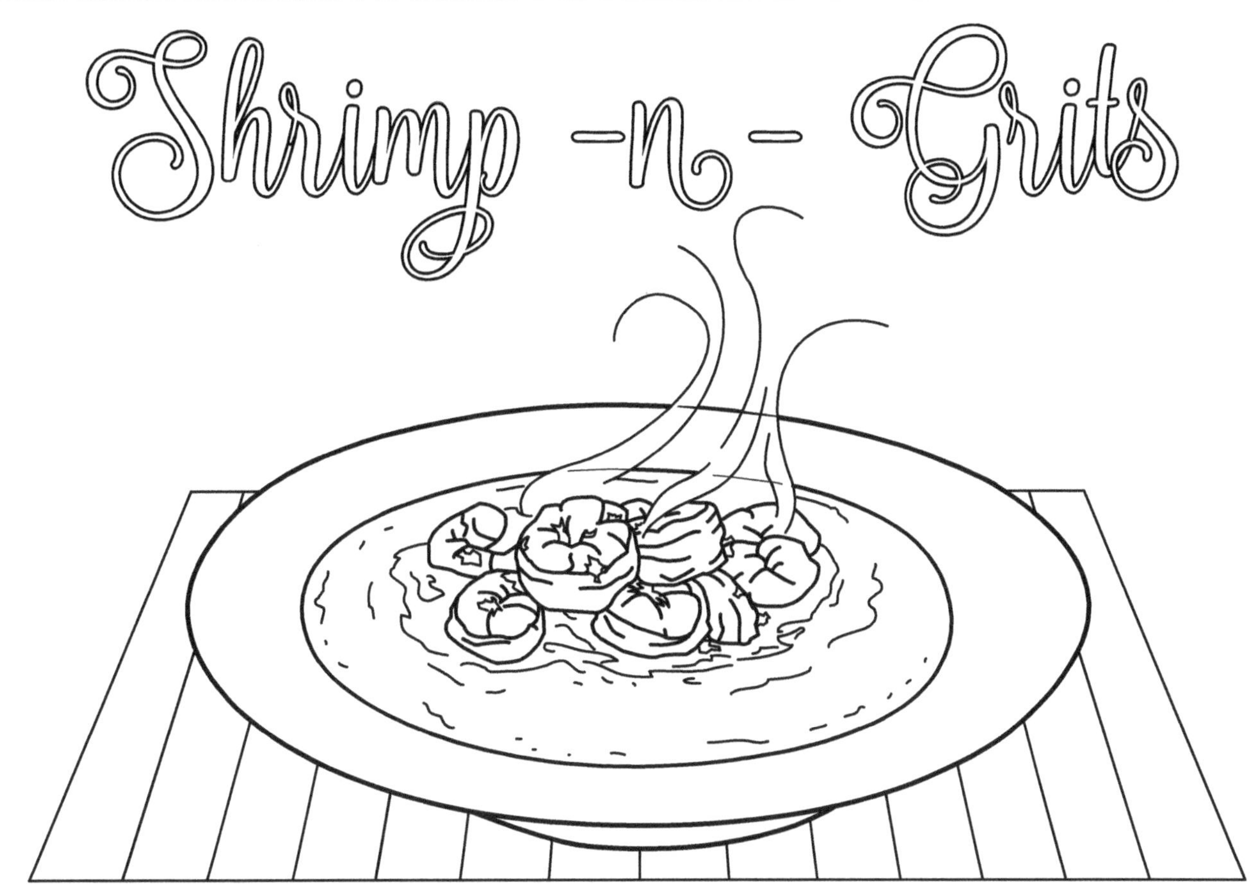

Grits

- 2 cups stone milled, organic white grits
- 4 cups 40% heavy cream
- 4 cups milk
- 4 cups water
- 1 stick unsalted whole butter
- Salt and white pepper to taste

Bring liquids and butter to rolling boil. Slowly add the grits, stirring constantly with wire whisk until brought back to boil. Lower heat to simmer. Simmer for 1/2 hour to 45 minutes, stirring occasionally with wooden spoon. Add salt and pepper.

Recipe Courtesy of

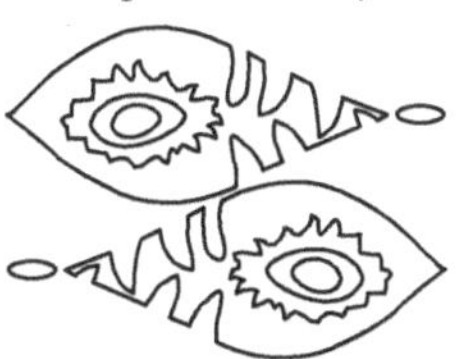

Shrimp, Toppings and Sauce

- 16 large fresh shrimp, peeled and de-veined
- 3 oz. red onion, diced small
- 3 oz. red and green bell pepper, diced small
- 3 oz. Andouille sausage, diced small
- 4 oz. fresh spinach, clipped and steams removed
- 1 cup white wine
- 1 cup heavy cream
- 1 oz. extra virgin olive oil
- Salt and pepper to taste

Heat a large sauté pan, add the olive oil. Season shrimp with salt and pepper and cook until transparent. Turn shrimp, add Andouille, onions and peppers to pan. Add white wine and cook to reduce by half. Add spinach leaves and cream and cook to reduce by half.

To Plate

Divide grits between 4 plates. Top with 4 shrimp per plate, tails up.

Divide sauce equally among plates. Serve immediately and enjoy!

Pisces Rising

Pisces Rising celebrates Florida cuisine since 2003. Their devotion is in farm-to-table practices delivered with passion and grace. The restaurant is lovingly wrapped around a Florida Cracker-style bungalow home built in the 1920s that gives off captivating Historic Florida vibes as soon as you step in. Enjoy an intimate dinner in the main dining room or on the outside deck watching the sunset over Lake Dora.

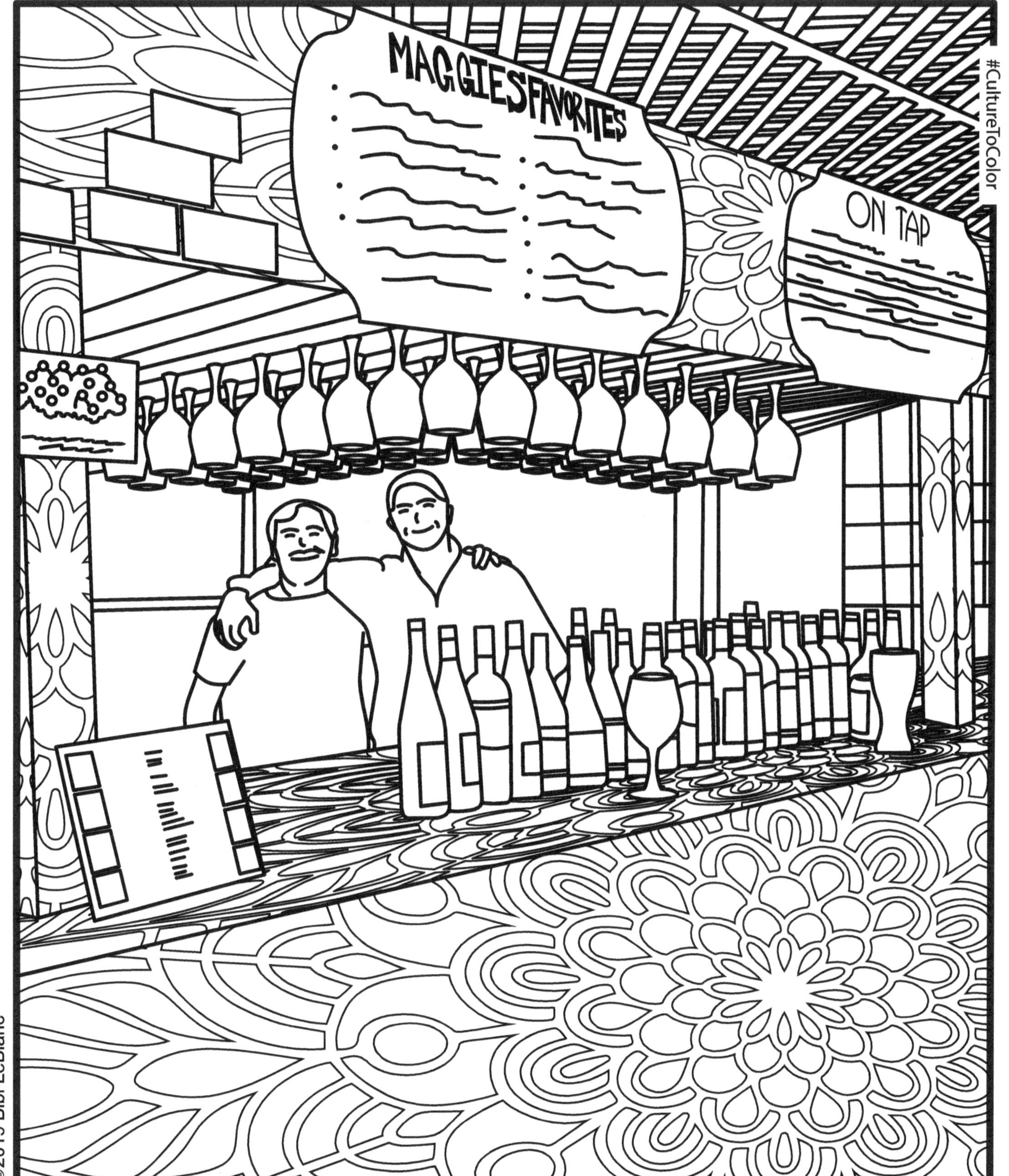

Maggie's Attic

Located in Historic Downtown Mount Dora, Maggie's Attic is a family-owned wine and beer cellar and eclectic boutique. Maggie's was established in 2003 with the goal of creating a fun, casual atmosphere in which guests could enjoy themselves while expanding their knowledge of wines and craft beers. Every day is a great day to stop by and relax with your favorite wine or beer. Cheers!

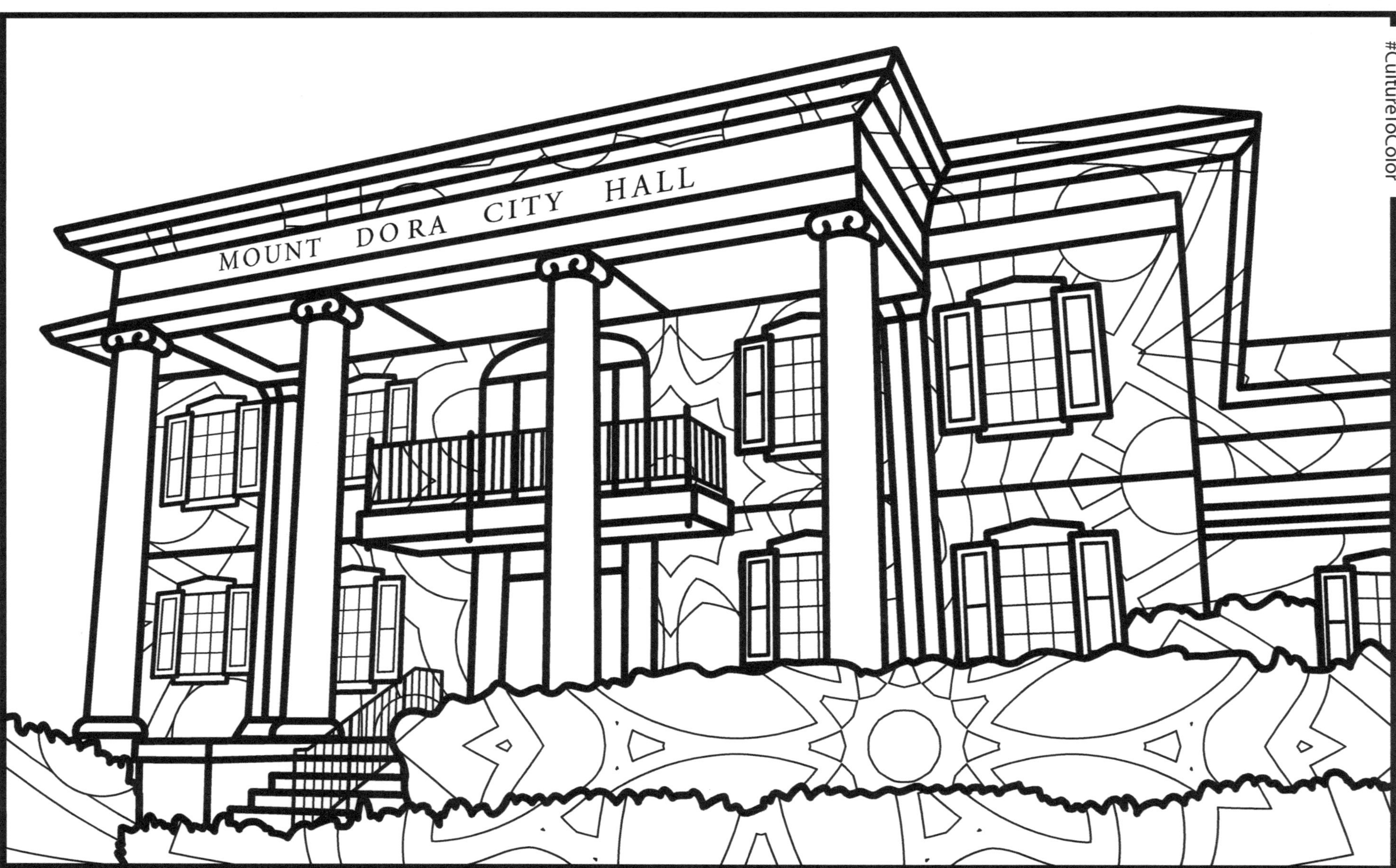

City Hall

The original Mount Dora City Hall was built in 1904 almost entirely by volunteer labor, from materials paid for by public donations. It was badly damaged by a fire in 1922. Today, Mount Dora City Hall, built by architect Brandon Wald, overlooks beautiful Donnelly Park and is one of the most beautiful city halls in Florida.

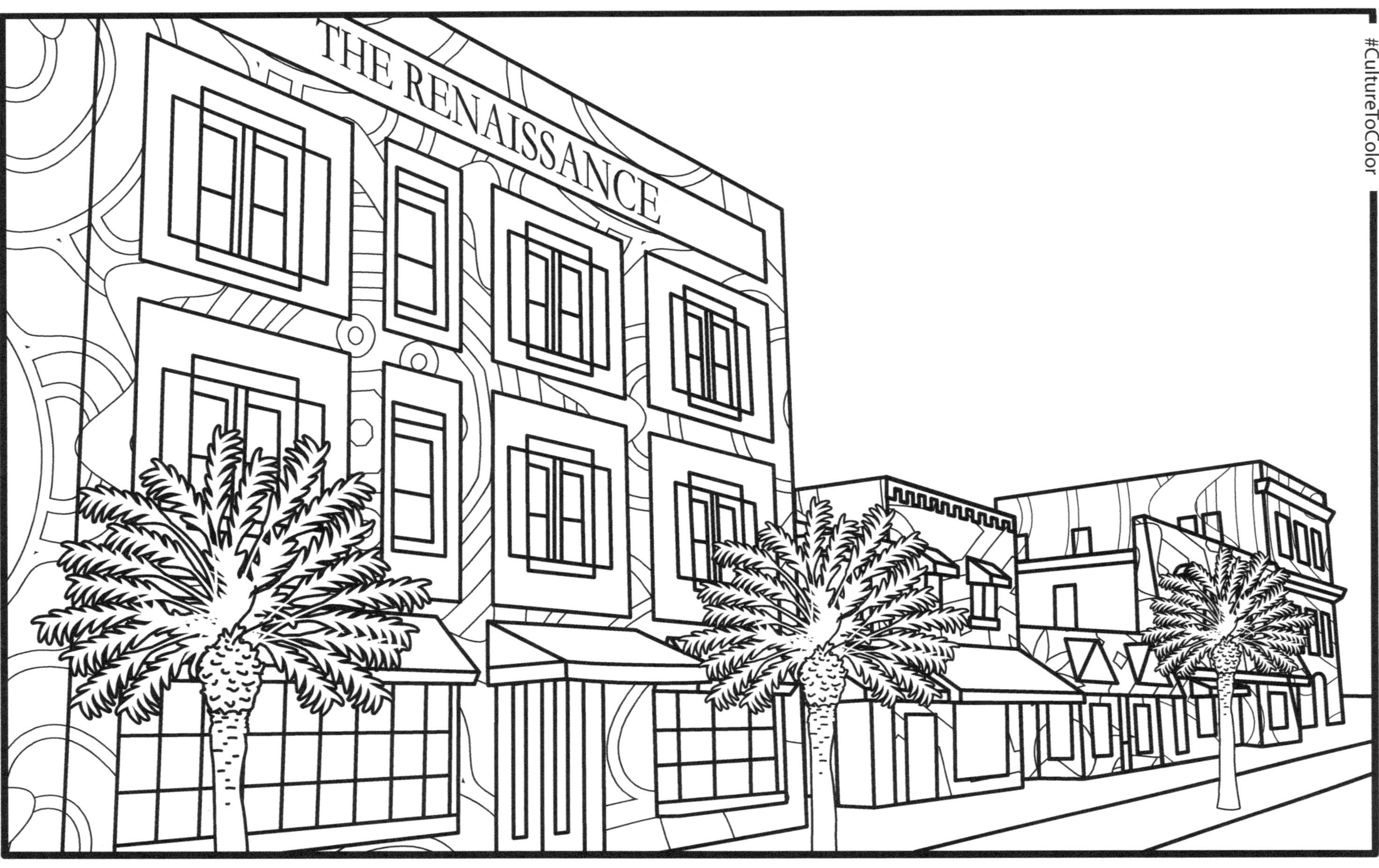

Historic Downtown - Donnelly Street

The Renaissance, a reputedly haunted grand hotel built in 1922, is home to an eclectic collection of stores and restaurants. Enjoy a coffee treat at the longest running coffee-shop, the Village Coffee Pot. Follow the scent of fresh teas and spices to The Spice & Tea Exchange. The whirling bubbles dancing along the sidewalk will lead you to Whispering Winds, a happy little gift shop. Come into Under the Cherry Blossoms for uplifting, functional artwork, jewelry, photography and much more featuring local artists.

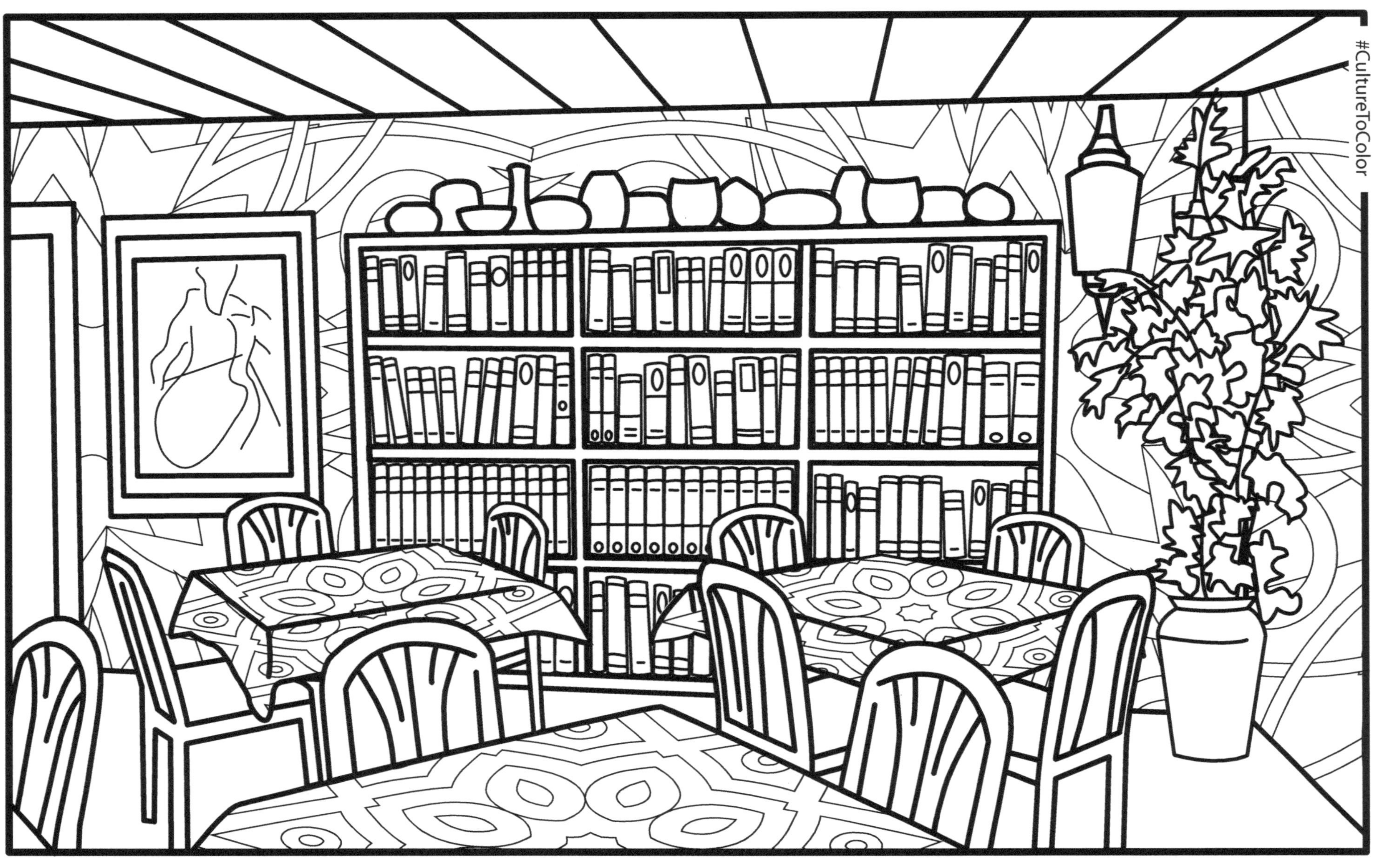

Goblin Market Restaurant & Lounge

A romantic hideaway of the highest order, Mount Dora's Goblin Market Restaurant is a favorite among critics both local and farther flung, not only for its eclectic menu, but its charming spaces, inside and out. Each of its three indoor dining rooms seems lifted from one of the books that line the walls, and although it's a well-known spot at this point, each visit feels as though you've stumbled upon something new, special, secret. Its outdoor space, too, has a quaint and clandestine vibe with lush Florida greenery to complement a decadent menu of lovingly homemade fare.

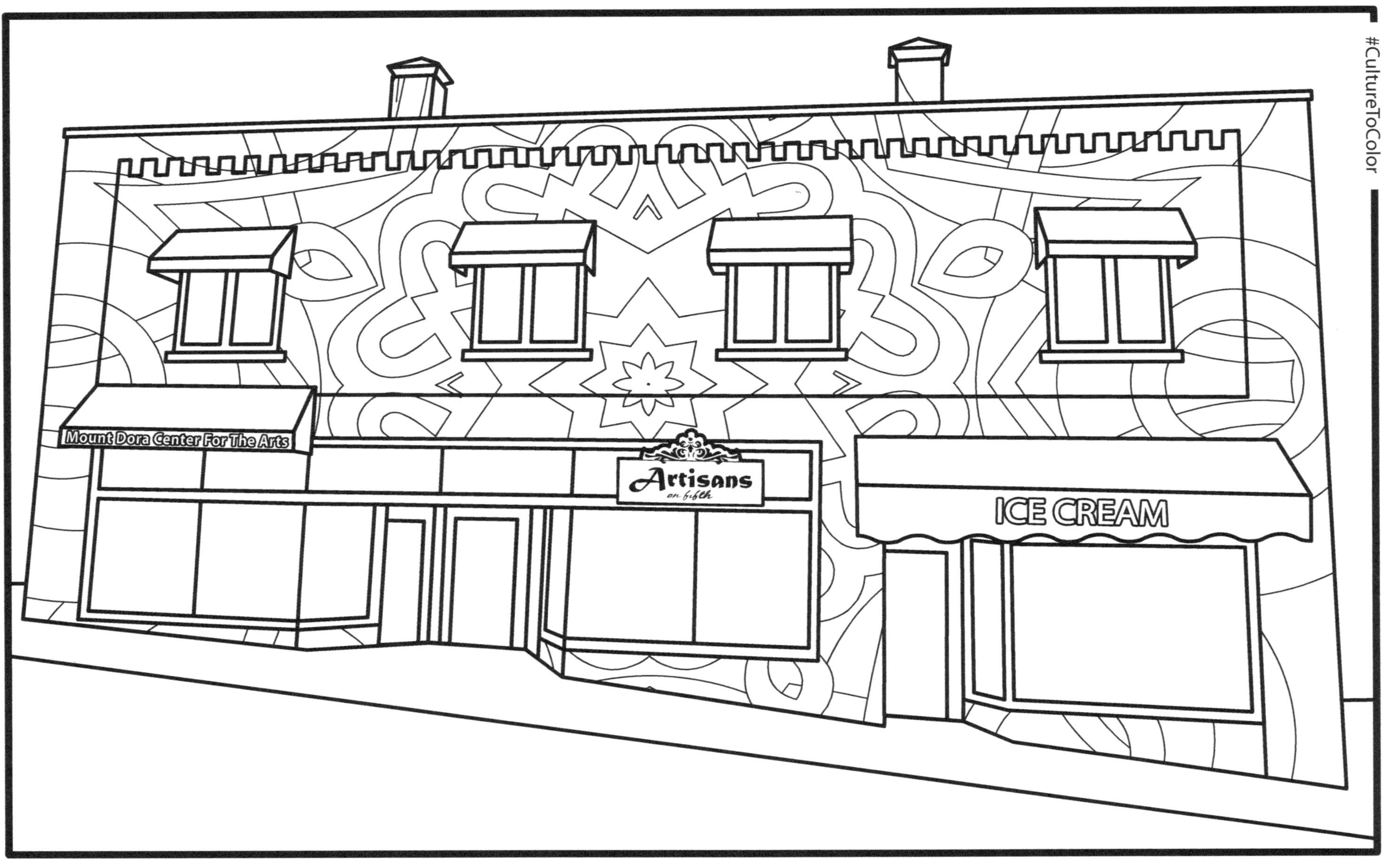

Center for the Arts

The Mount Dora Center for the Arts was founded by a group of volunteers who wanted to celebrate the arts in Mount Dora. Today, it is a multifaceted community center. It serves the community by fostering an understanding and appreciation of art and culture through diverse exhibits of original art, educational programs for adults and children, outreach programs, Kids Summer Arts Camp, and the nationally recognized Mount Dora Arts Festival!

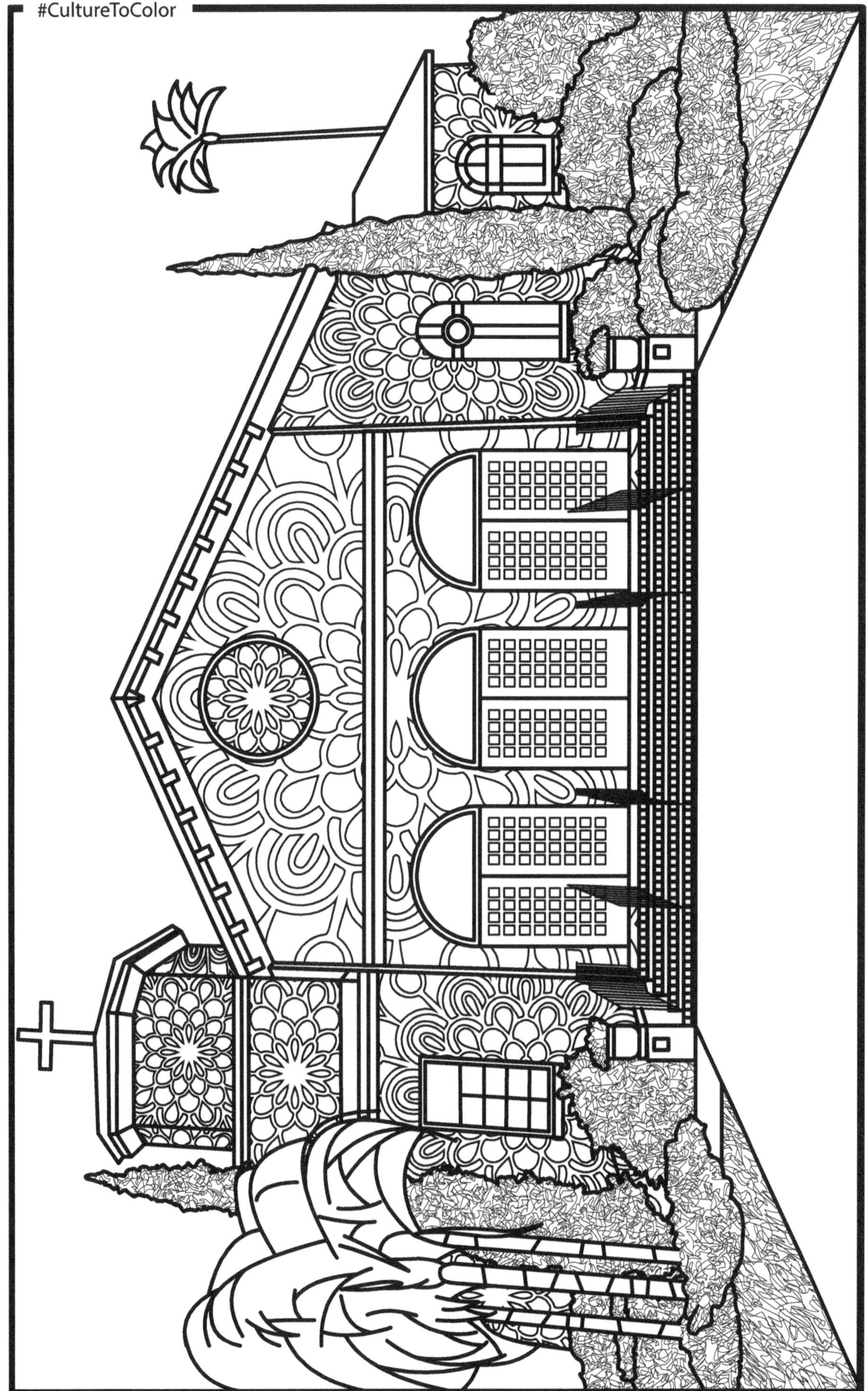

First United Methodist Church of Mount Dora

In 1880, Mount Dora was a place of timber, lakes, and a small community of people with no churches. The Methodists began gathering for prayer meetings and Sunday school. The minister was a traveling circuit-riding pastor who led worship every few months. In January 1884, the time had come to build a church building. Today, the congregation has gone through many changes and expansions. But the tradition of regular prayer meetings, Sunday school, and worship continues. Ministries to children and students nurture the next generation of believers.

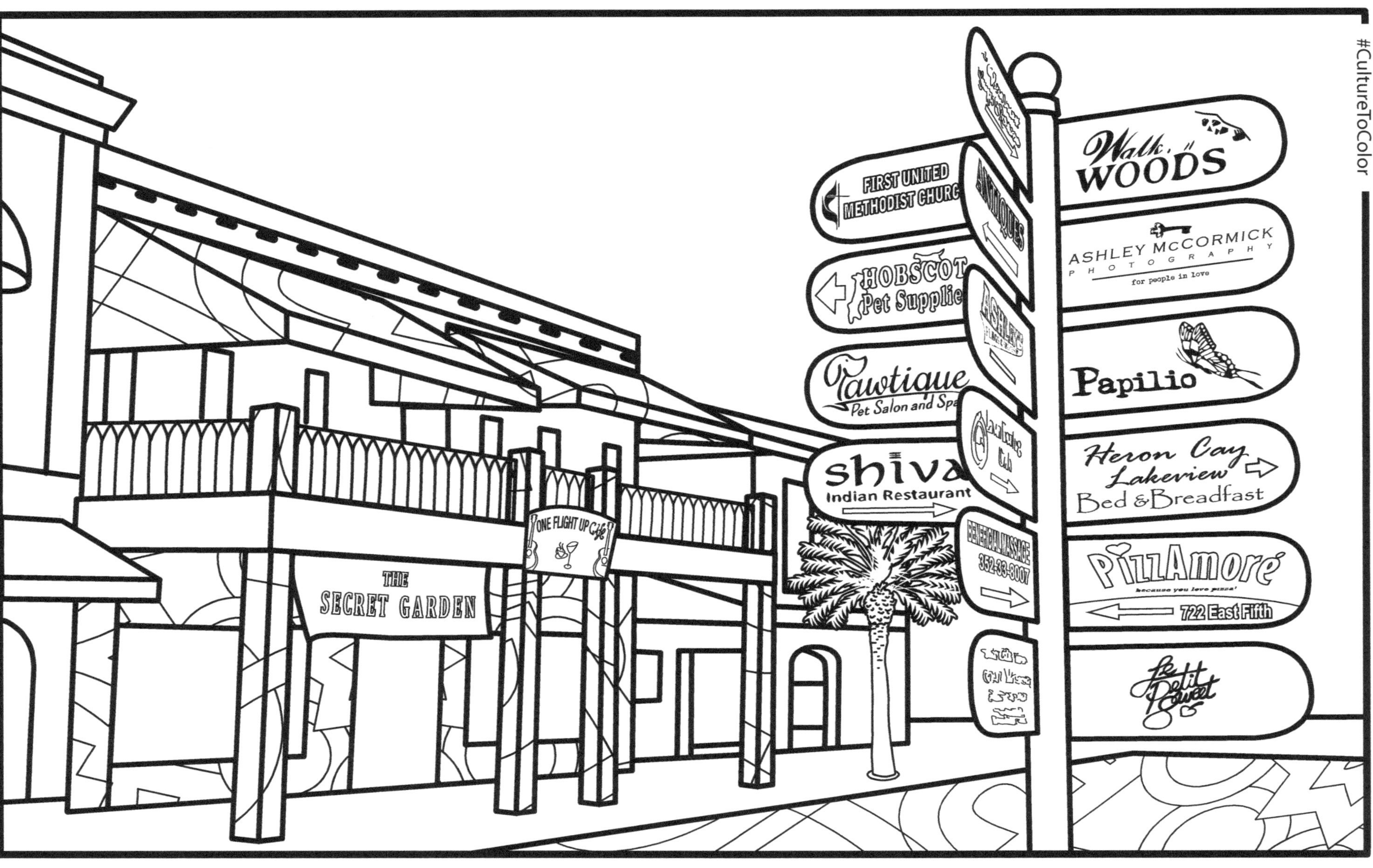

One Flight Up & Wayfinder

The Mount Dora Wayfinding Signs make it easy to find Downtown businesses and points of interest. When you enter through the doors of The Secret Garden, you can't help but feel the romance of the 1920s in this Parisian-inspired jewel of Mount Dora! The Secret Garden boutique is truly a special place. Ready for a break from shopping? One Flight Up, a local favorite, offers coffee, light fare, wine and beer. Get a great view of the hustle and bustle of Downtown Mount Dora from their shady balcony overlooking Donnelly Street.

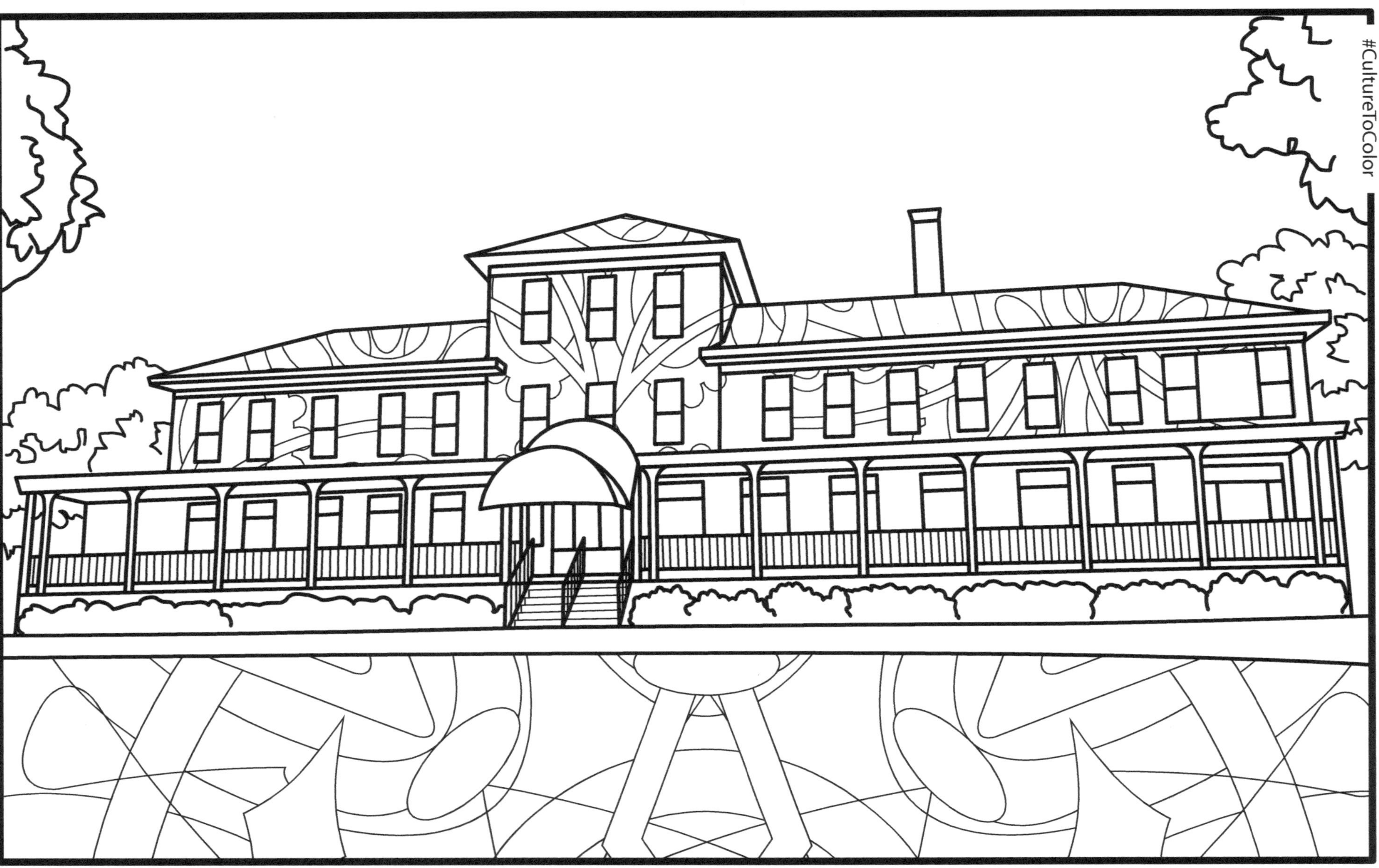

©2019 Bibi LeBlanc

Lakeside Inn

Pass through the stone gateposts of Lakeside Inn and you will instantly step back in time. Florida's Most Historic Hotel, built in 1883, is the oldest continuously operated hotel in Florida. The last of the grand Victorian era hotels, it has hosted many noted dignitaries and celebrities, including President Calvin Coolidge and first lady Grace Coolidge. Enjoy the hotel's timeless setting for a relaxing getaway, your special occasion or event. Wander acres of beautifully landscaped grounds, with moss-draped oak trees, sweeping down to the pool and white-sand shoreline of Lake Dora.

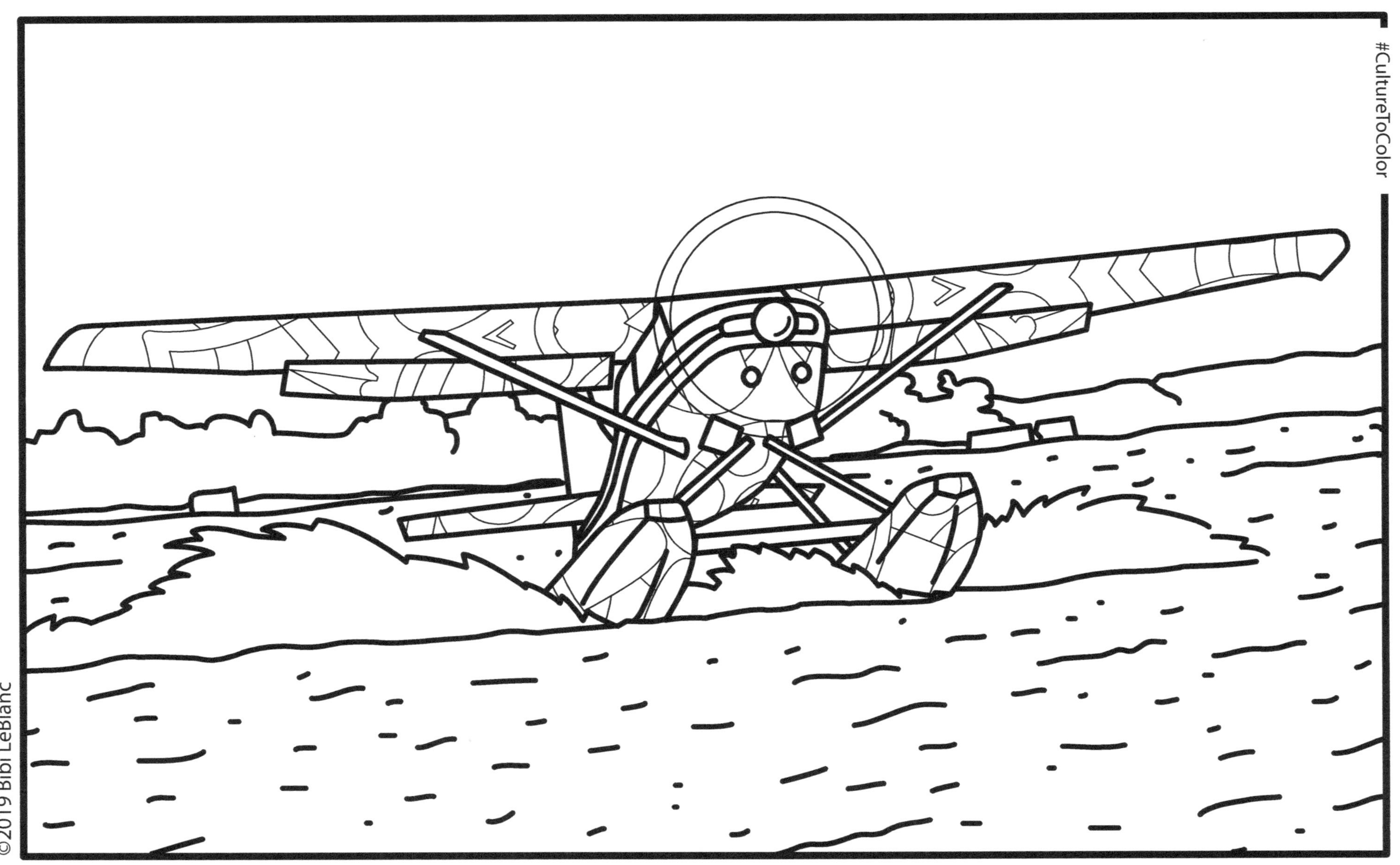

Jones Brothers Air and Seaplane Adventures

Take flight and enjoy the breathtaking views across the vast areas of lakes Harris and Griffin on the way to the wilderness of the Ocklawaha River and Ocala National Forest. Then turn back across lakes Yale and Eustis just in time for a flight straight into the sunset across Lake Dora. Jones Brothers offers seaplane adventure tours around Central Florida, including seaplane barhops, dinners, lunches, breakfasts at the springs, wedding proposals and wedding flights. Jones Brothers is also a Gold Seal Certified flight school offering seaplane instruction.

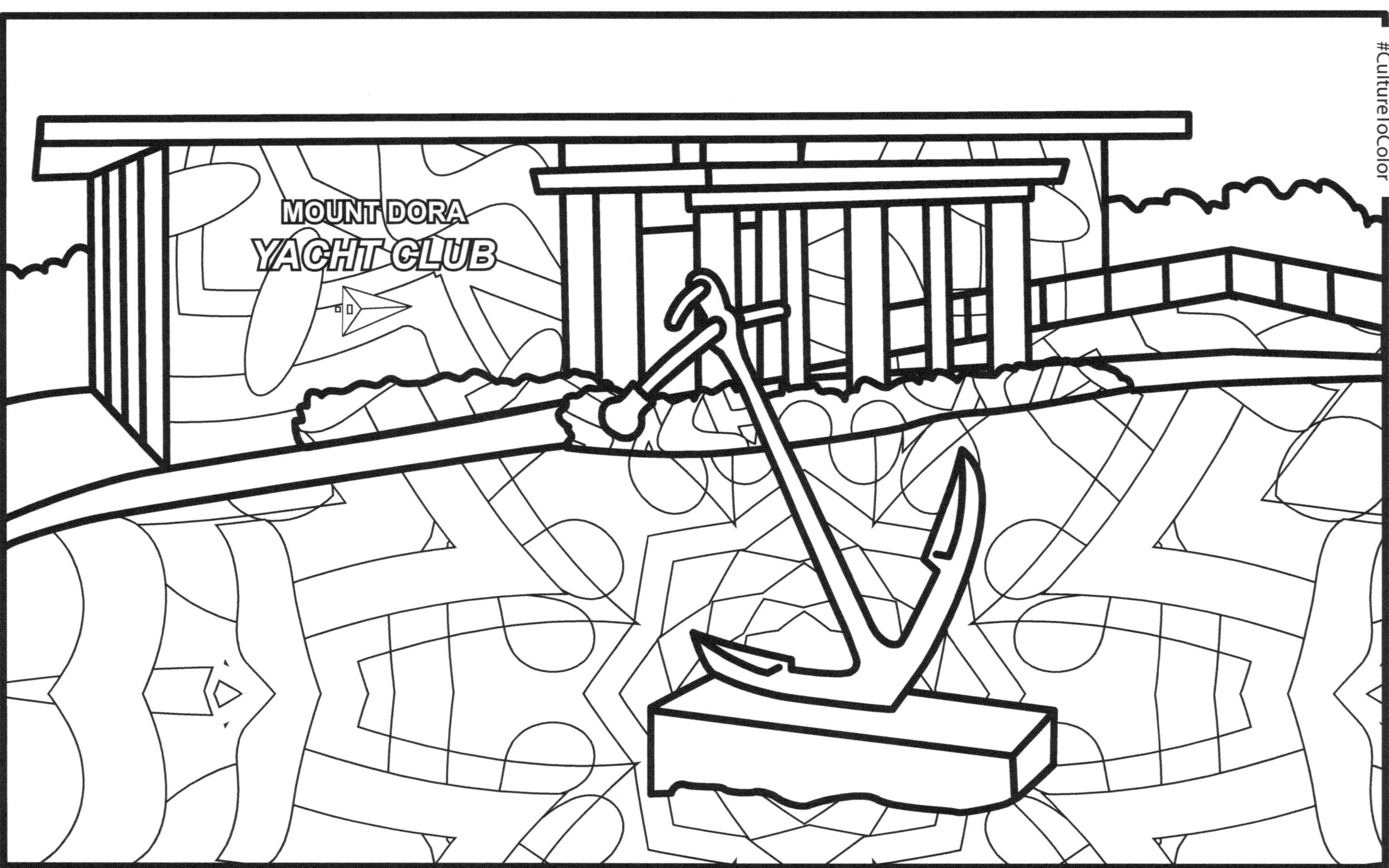

Yacht Club

The Mount Dora Yacht Club, established in 1913, is Florida's oldest inland-waterway yacht club. Located in the heart of beautiful Downtown Mount Dora, it offers spectacular views of sunsets over Lake Dora. Every spring, members still organize the annual Mount Dora Sailing Regatta for two days of racing. 2019 marks the 66th year of the regatta, the city's longest-running annual event.

Old Joe

Old Joe is a 15-foot, 1,200-pound bronze alligator. "On Lake Dora, at the turn of the 19th century, an alligator named Old Joe could be seen cruising these waters. The captains of the paddle-wheel boats would point out Old Joe, the largest, fiercest and most respected alligator on the lake. It was said that he would eat not only fish but also deer and other large animals. Today, when you see an alligator, you are seeing one of Old Joe's offspring. Like him, they are dangerous and are to be respected. This statue is for your enjoyment. Please leave the real ones alone!"

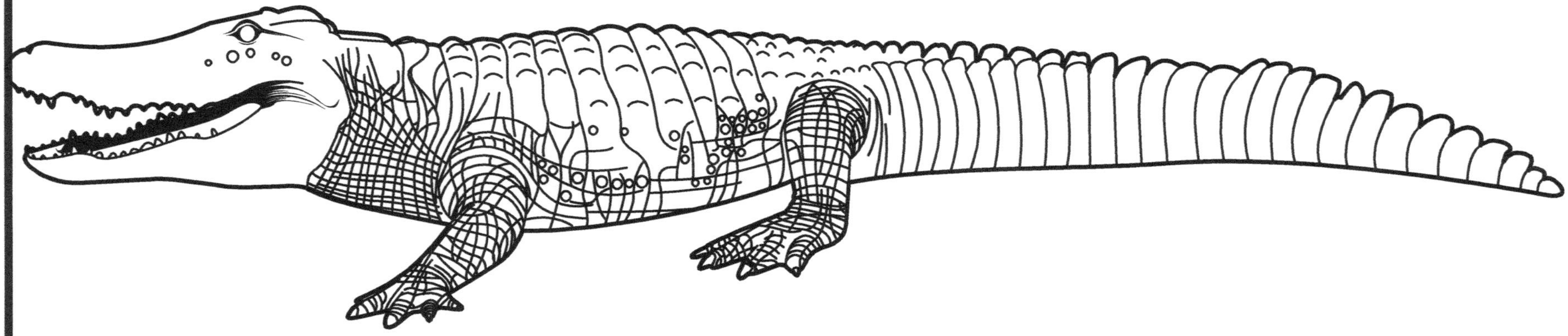

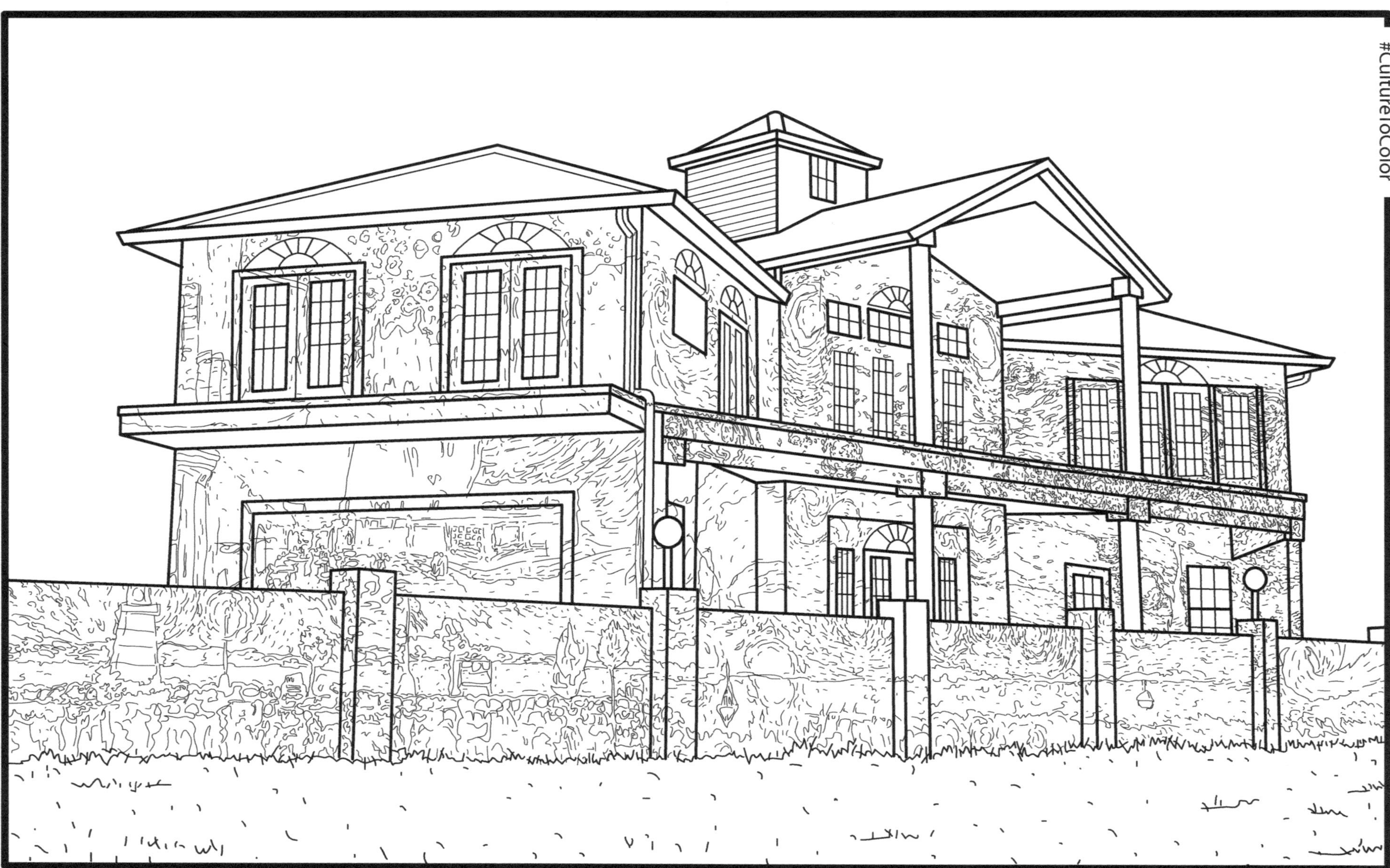

Starry Night House

The inspiration behind the original mural at the Starry Night House was autism. People with autism can have limited verbal skills and a tendency to wander. The owners commissioned the murals on the exterior walls to serve as a landmark for their autistic son, who loves van Gogh's work. It calms and comforts him. Should he wander and be unable to communicate clearly, he can mention the Starry Night House, and people are able to help bring him home. The original "Starry Night," painted in 1889 in oil on canvas, is displayed at the Museum of Modern Art in New York City.

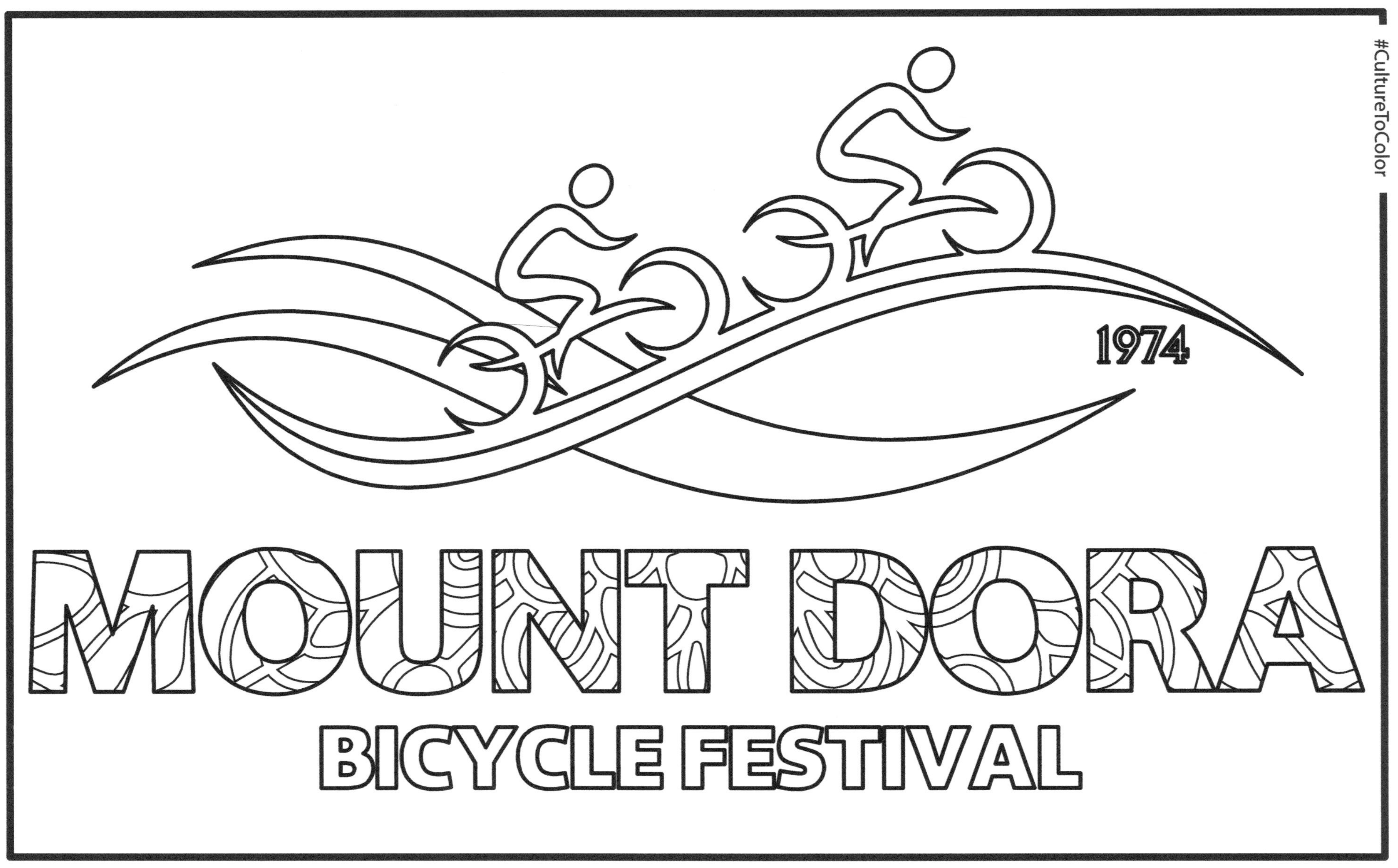

Bicycle Festival

The annual Mount Dora Bicycle Festival celebrates all things cycling: no matter how fast or slow or what kind of bike you ride, tandems, hand cycles, road bikes, mountain bikes, hybrids, cruisers and recumbent bikes. The Bicycle Festival & Gran Fondo is Florida's only four-day Premier Cycling Social. Choose from up to 16 routes, with optional Gran Fondo challenges. Routes are designed to challenge any ride level, while offering beautiful scenery through three counties.

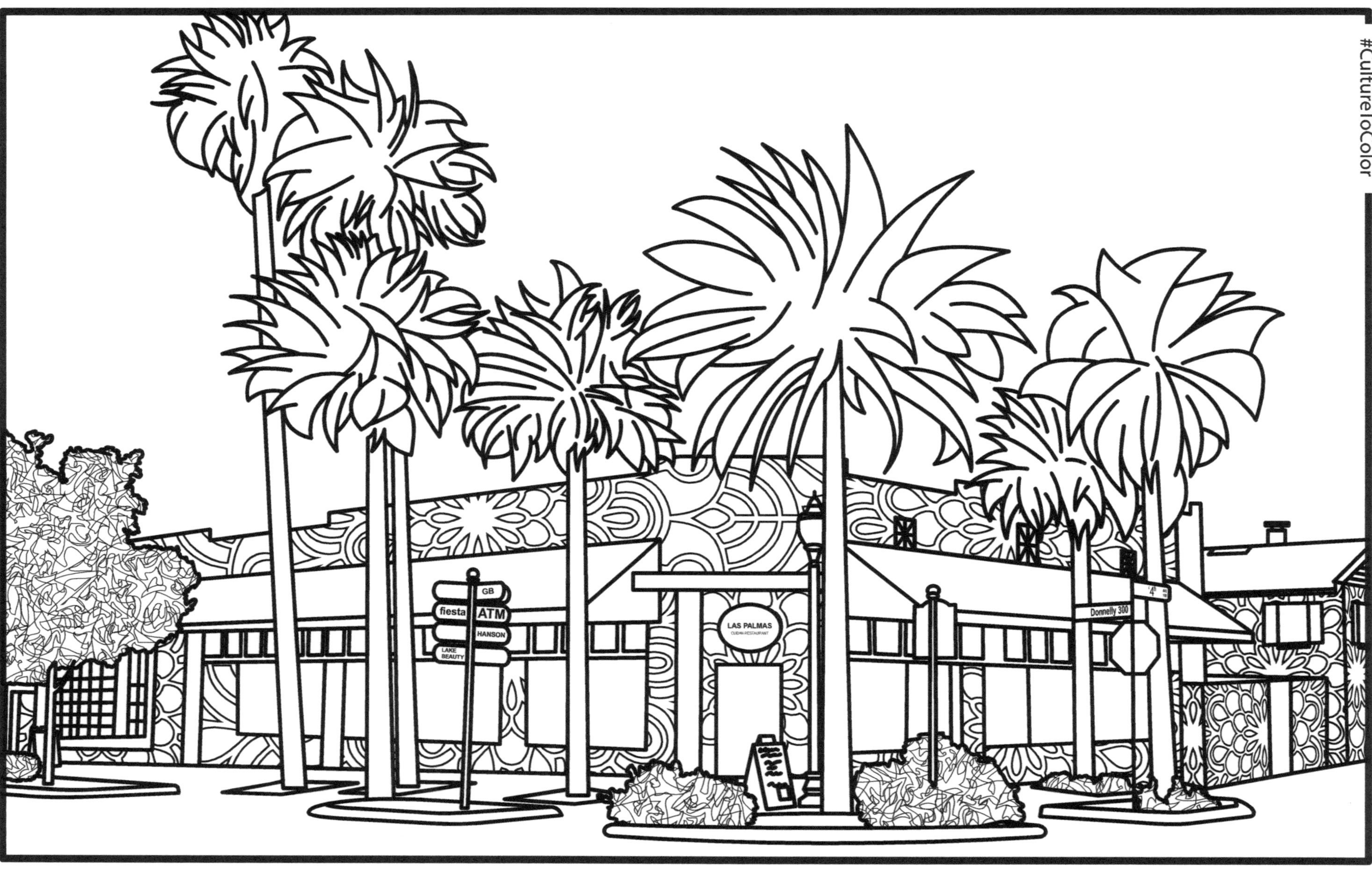

Las Palmas Cuban Restaurant

Las Palmas Cuban Restaurant is passionate about their authentic Cuban food. You will feel transported into the tropics as you dine at Las Palmas Cuban Restaurant. Whether you are looking for a place to dine with family, hang out with friends or bring that special someone for a romantic dinner, Las Palmas Cuban Restaurant is the place to be. Sit back, relax and enjoy your visit to a taste of Cuba.

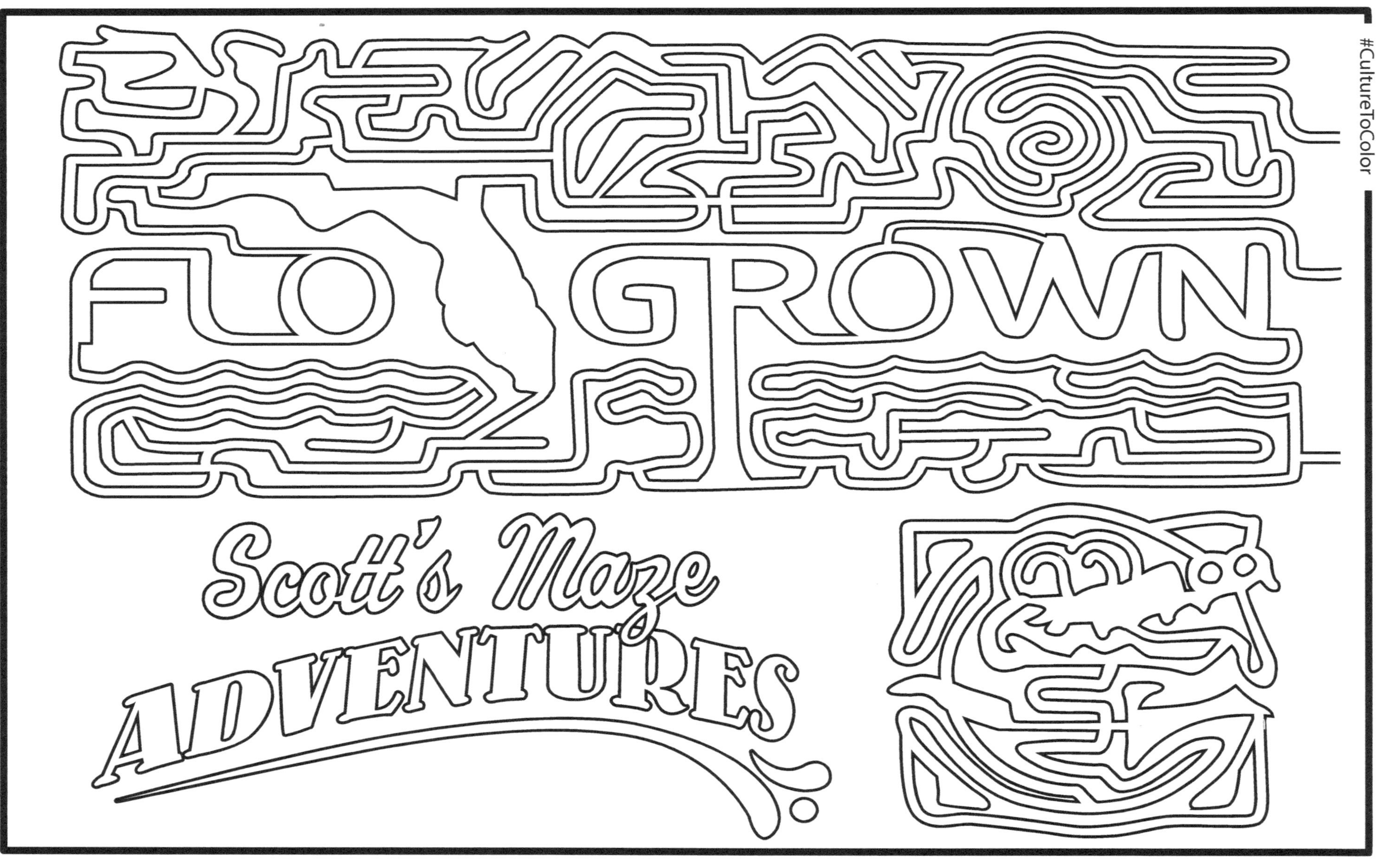

Long and Scott Farms – Maze Adventures

It all started with just a 7-acre cornfield... Now it has become a tradition with many visitors. It's a maze, it's a game, it's educational, and it's FUN! Year after year, each corn maze has a unique design, with twisting pathways, questions and answers, and picture rubbings. Come get LOST! Take your friends and family to see who can navigate the maze the quickest!

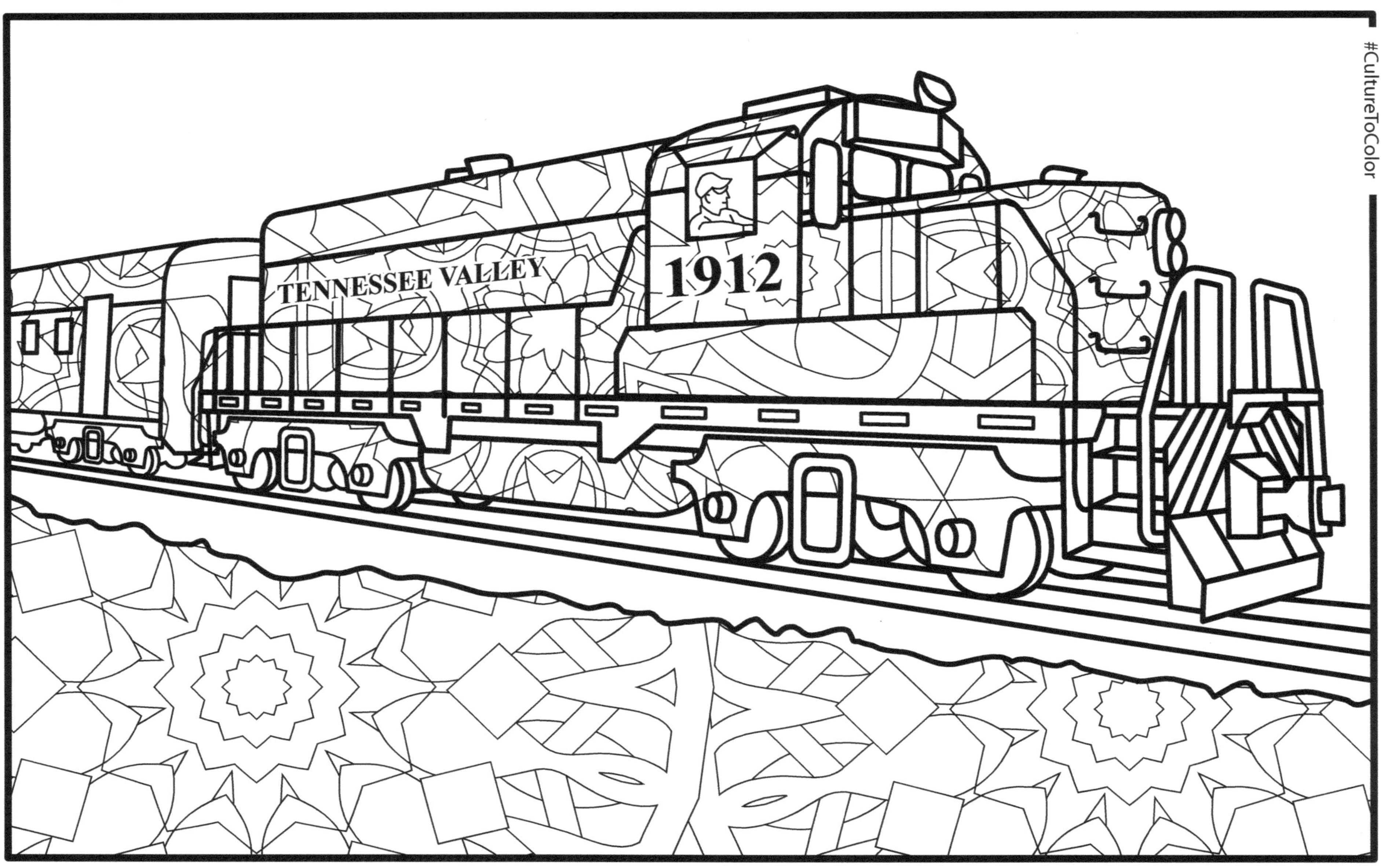

The Royal Palm Railway Experience

Hop on board the fleet of beautifully restored, 1940s vintage passenger cars for a journey back in time, when famous passenger trains with names like The Champion, Southern Crescent, Southwind and the Royal Palm, crossed the nation. Solve a "Murder on the Royal Palm" or choose from other excursions like The Royal Pizza Express, Rails & Ales, or The Polar Express™ at Christmastime. In decades past, passengers enjoyed riding through the countryside in coaches, sleeping cars, lounges and diners that were at the height of efficiency, comfort and beauty! Now, you can, too!

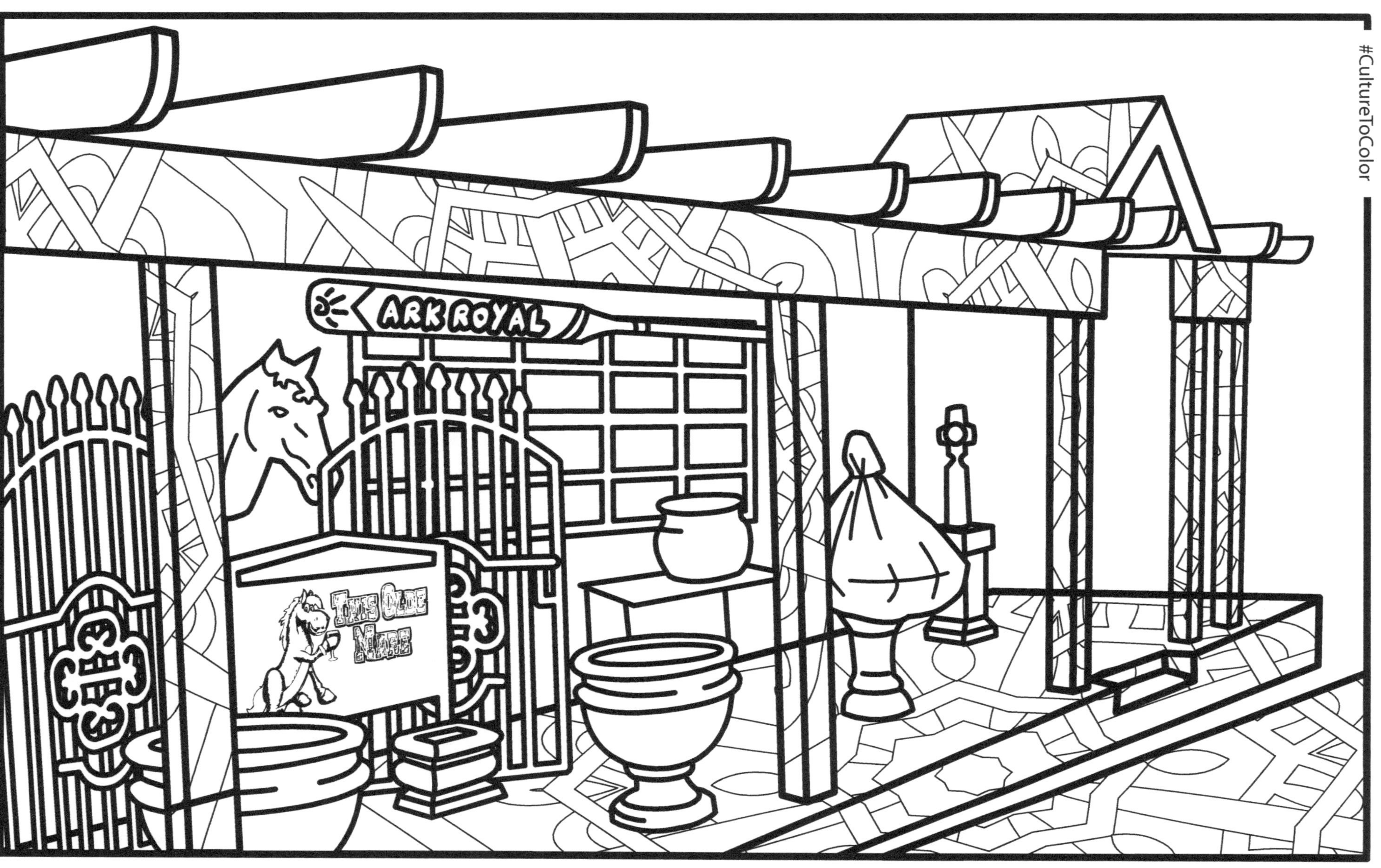

Renninger's Antique Center, Flea & Farmer's Market

If you have been searching for antique and vintage furniture, paintings, jewelry, decorative art, shabby chic, collectibles and thousands of other items, you can find them at Renninger's Antique Center. Renninger's, the largest source of antiques in the Southeast, has more than 180 indoor shops. There is also a consignment area with 20 booths and 40 cases. Dealers outside, and in the Street of Shops, also sell the above items. Renninger's Flea and Farmer's Market in Mount Dora is home to hundreds of dealers who sell just about anything you could imagine.

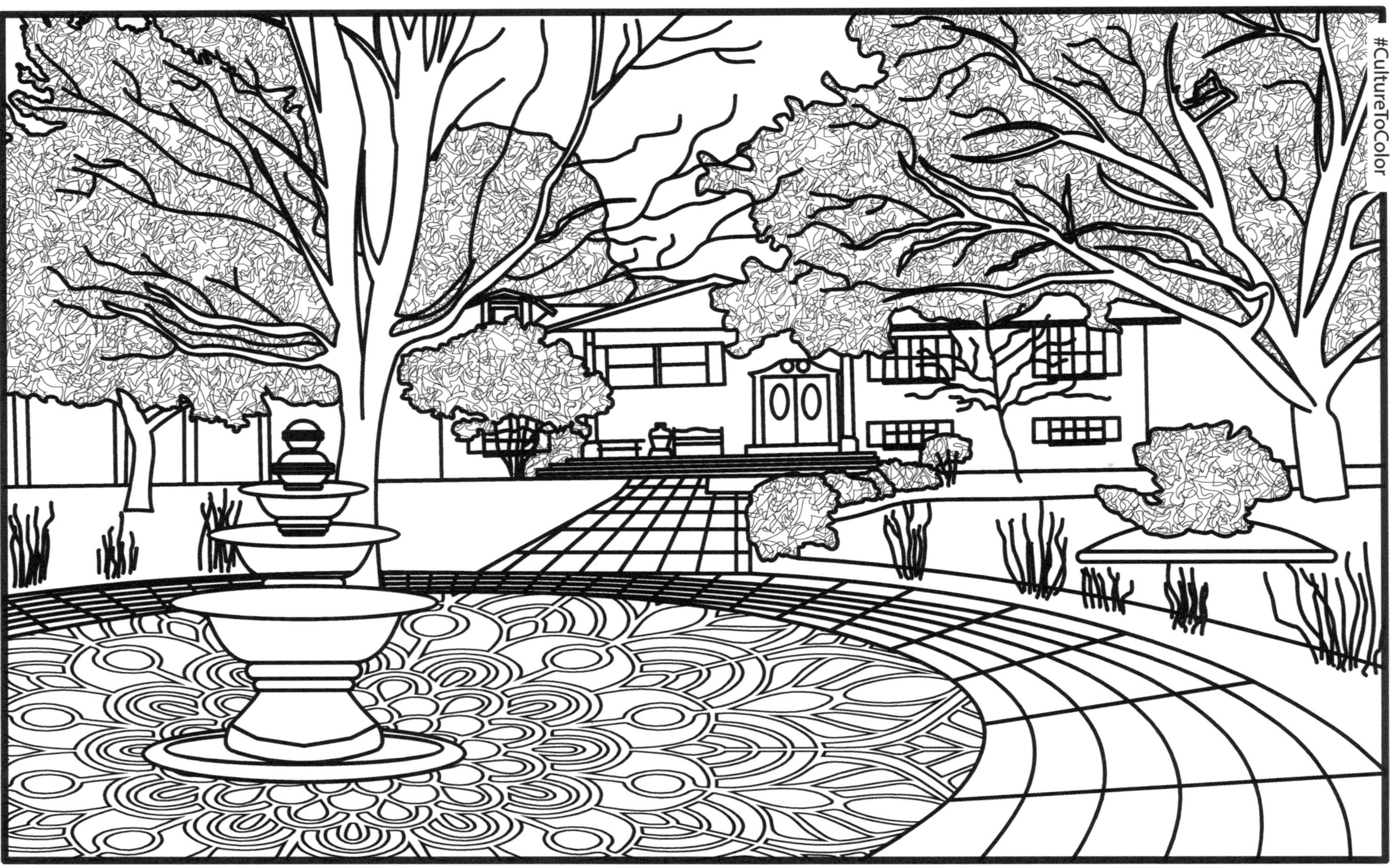

Amy's Flower Patch Farm Bed & Breakfast

Amy's Flower Patch Farm is an oasis just outside Mount Dora, complete with an art studio and gift shop that houses some of Amy Sellers' art work and historical items. They are all contained on acres of magnificent grounds to help guests unwind and recharge. Amy considers art in its many forms a gift from God that helps memorialize those unique spaces in time where we create our memories. Amy and her family are thrilled to share her next work of art with their guests to make more wonderful memories!

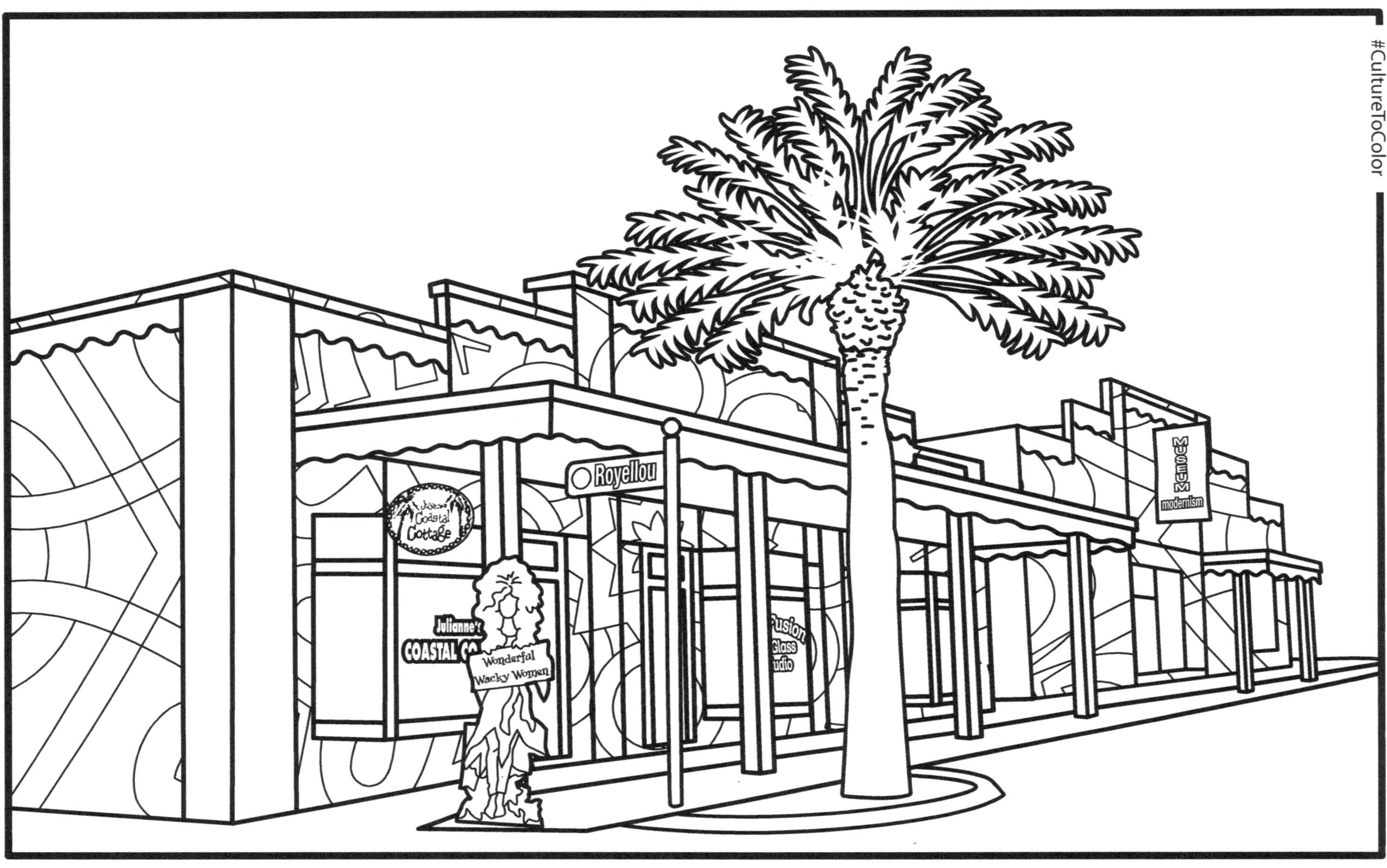

Historic Downtown with Modernism Museum

This stretch of Fourth Avenue in Downtown Mount Dora is home to Julianne's Coastal Cottage, an eclectic boutique with everything Florida, and, everyone's favorite, frozen wine slushy samples. If you would like to have a special, one-of-a-kind dinnerware pattern created just for you, stop in at Lee Fusion Art Glass Studio. The Modernism Museum explores the work of artists who found new expressive possibilities in the field of functional objects. Explore the unique collection, and experience Modernism in a way you won't find anywhere else.

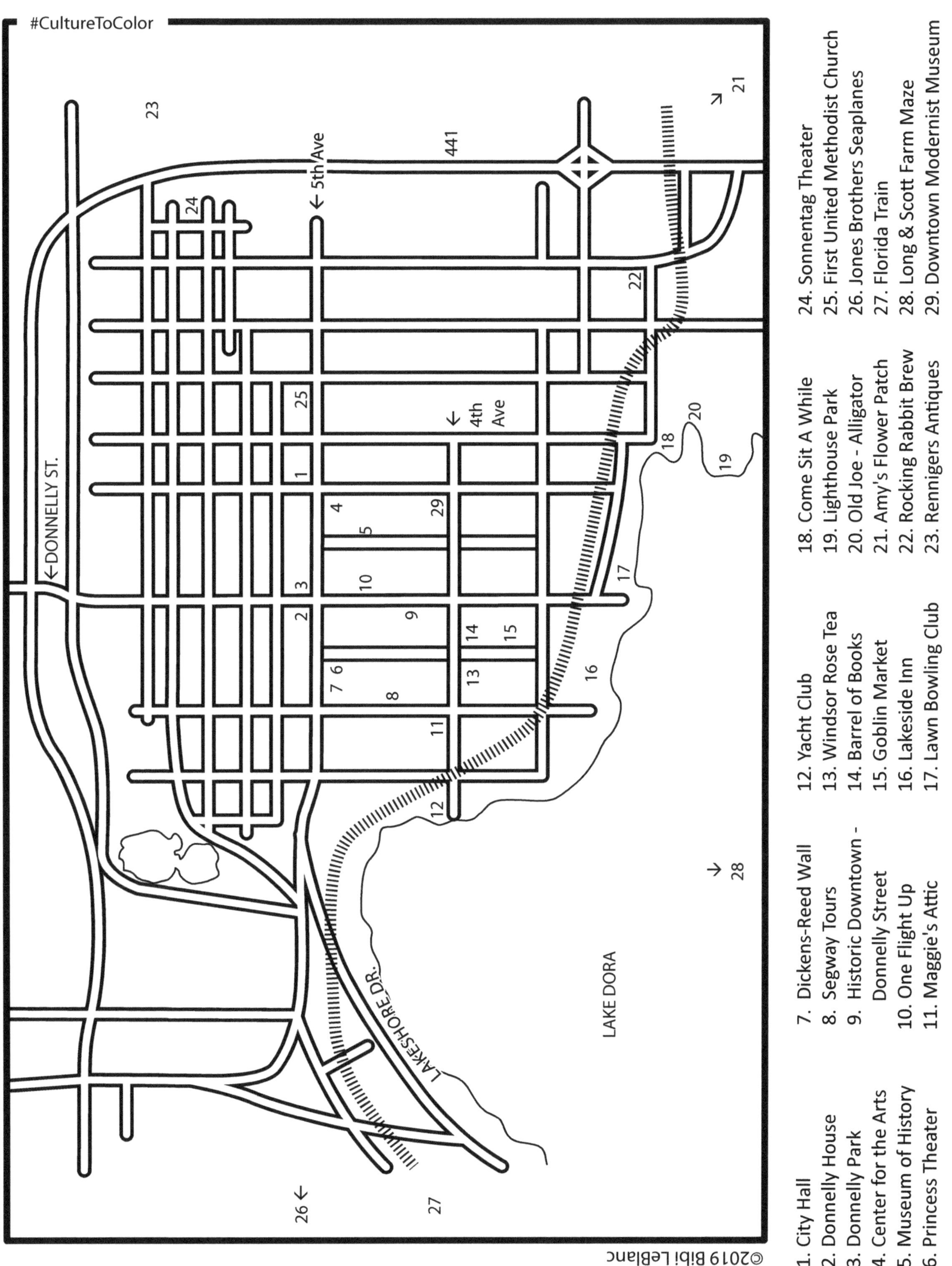

©2019 Bibi LeBlanc

1. City Hall
2. Donnelly House
3. Donnelly Park
4. Center for the Arts
5. Museum of History
6. Princess Theater
7. Dickens-Reed Wall
8. Segway Tours
9. Historic Downtown - Donnelly Street
10. One Flight Up
11. Maggie's Attic
12. Yacht Club
13. Windsor Rose Tea
14. Barrel of Books
15. Goblin Market
16. Lakeside Inn
17. Lawn Bowling Club
18. Come Sit A While
19. Lighthouse Park
20. Old Joe - Alligator
21. Amy's Flower Patch
22. Rocking Rabbit Brew
23. Rennigers Antiques
24. Sonnentag Theater
25. First United Methodist Church
26. Jones Brothers Seaplanes
27. Florida Train
28. Long & Scott Farm Maze
29. Downtown Modernist Museum

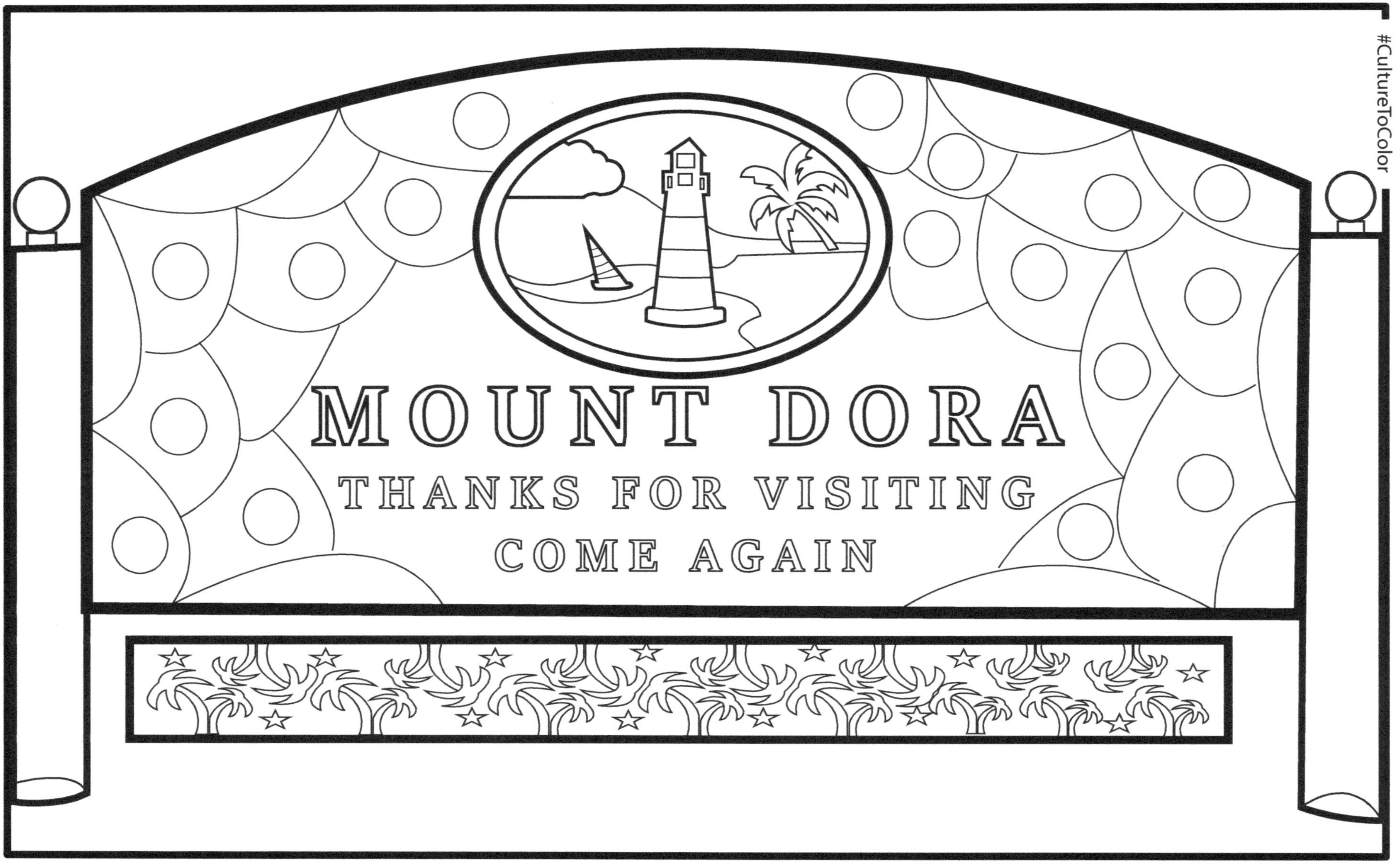

Thank You for Visiting – Come Again

Thank you for visiting Mount Dora. This historic town in Central Florida is truly "Someplace Special," and we are glad you came!

Vielen Dank * Taing a thoirt * Merci * Gracias * Mahalo
* Tak * Dank je * ευχαριστώ * Takk * Grazie

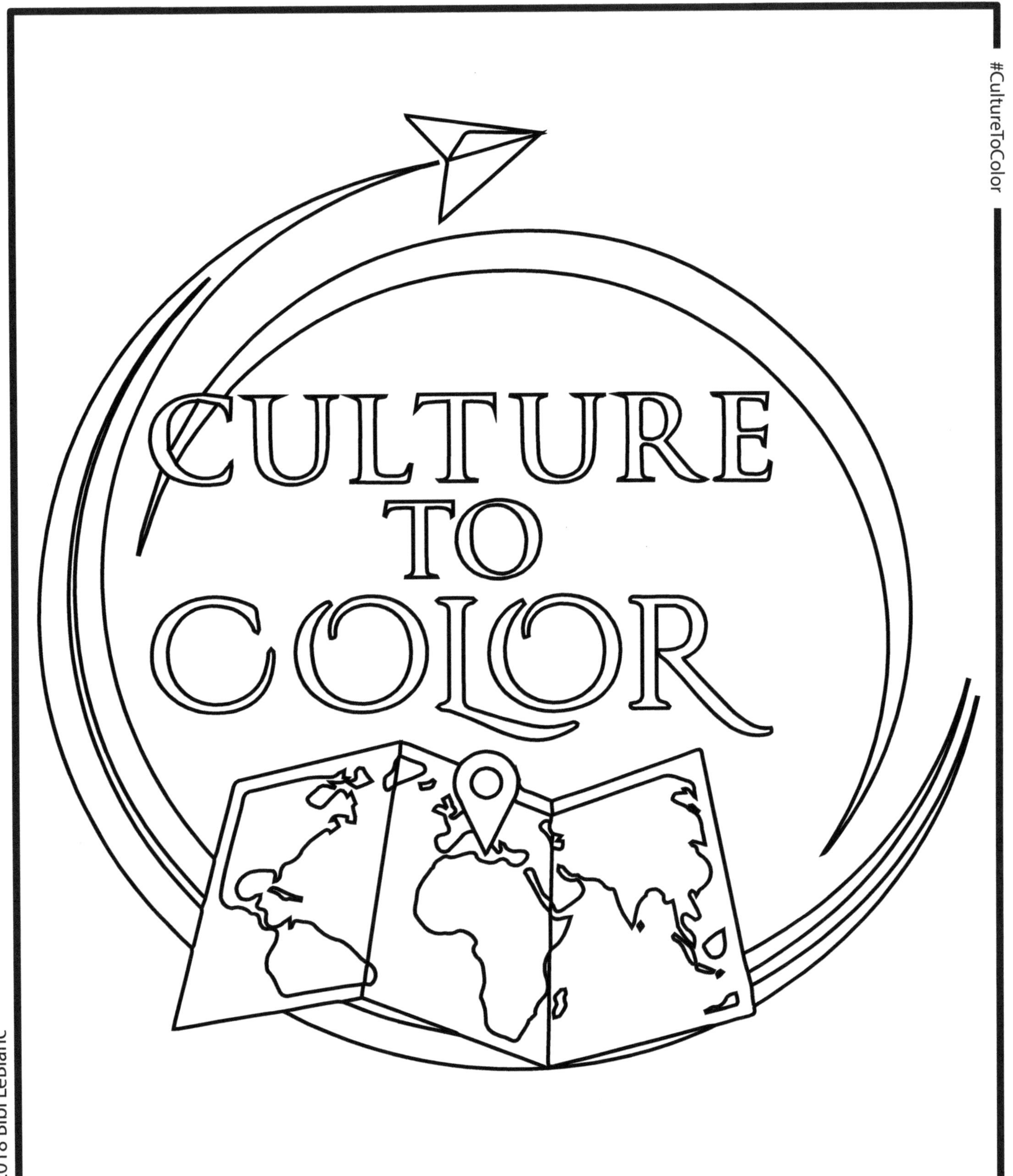

Culture to Color

Coloring Books that combine History & Fun Art for ages 5 – 105.
"Coloring Adventures around the Globe. No suitcase necessary!"

THANK YOU

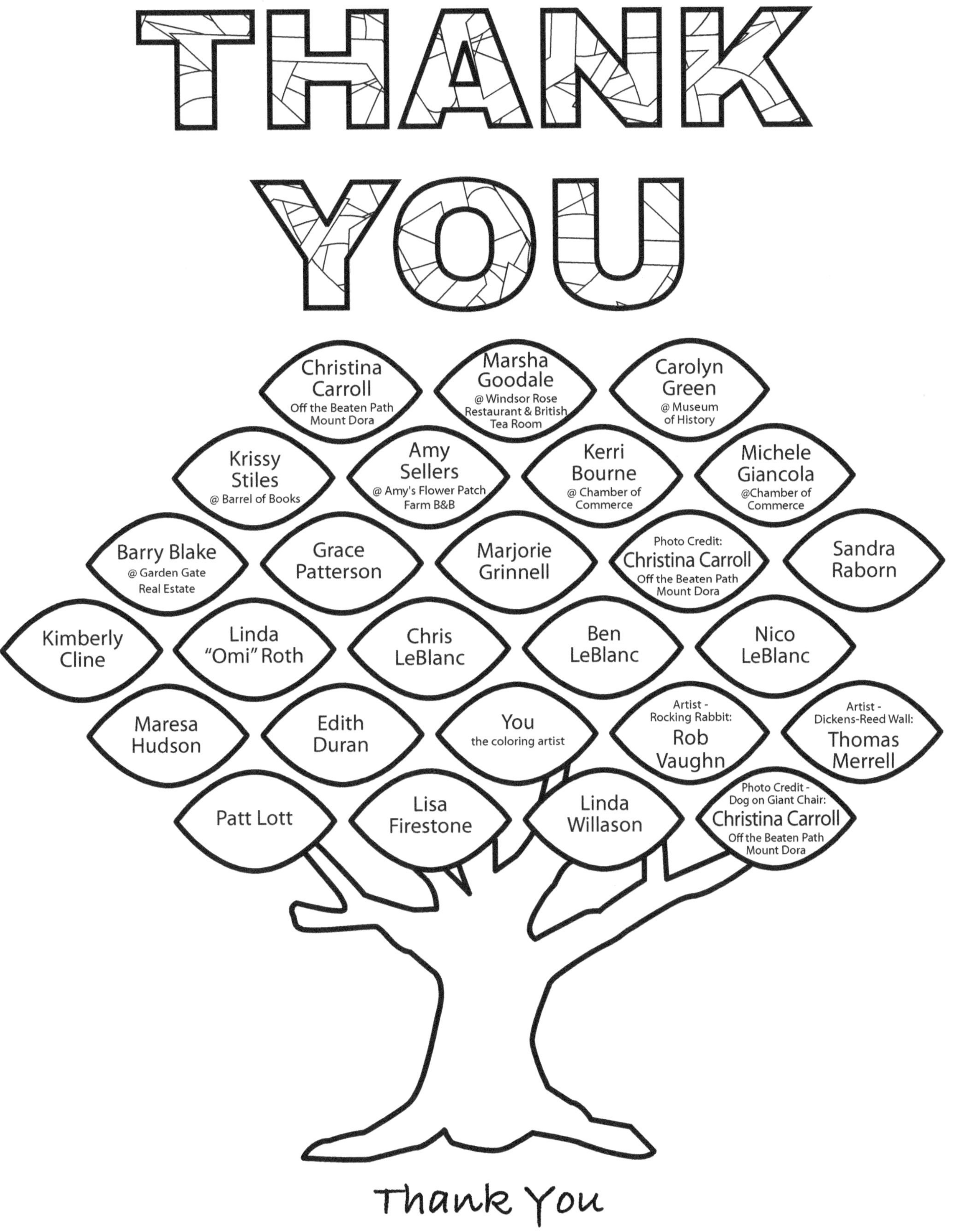

It has been so interesting and fun to explore & discover & meet the people of Mount Dora!
Thank you to everyone who has helped me make this Mount Dora Coloring Book a reality. I hope you enjoy coloring it as much as I did creating it!

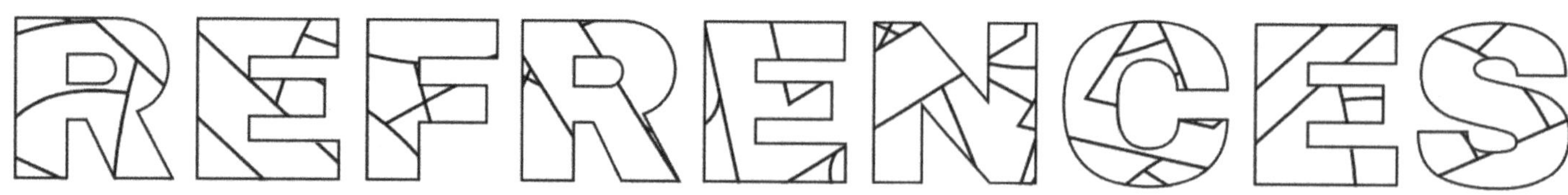

REFRENCES

Amy's Flower Patch Farm Bed & Breakfast:
>amysflowerpatchfarm.com

Barrel of Books and Games:
>barrelofbooksandgames.com

Center for the Arts:
>mountdoracenterforthearts.org

City Hall:
>ci.mount-dora.fl.us

City of Mount Dora Pipe Band and Scottish Highland Festival:
>cityofmtdorapipeband.com
>facebook.com/cityofmtdorapipeband
>visitscotland.com/info/towns-villages/forres-p237691

Come Sit a While - Grantham Point Park:
>ci.mount-dora.fl.us/904/Parks

Culture To Color:
>culturetocolor.com

Donnelly Park:
>ci.mount-dora.fl.us/Facilities/Facility/Details/Donnelly-Park-Building-Deck-Pad-13
>usapa.org

First United Methodist Church:
>mtdorafumc.org

Goblin Market Restaurant & Lounge:
>goblinmarketrestaurant.com

Historic Downtown – Donnelly Street:
>villagecoffeepot.com
>spiceandtea.com/mountdora
>whisperingwindsmountdora.com
>facebook.com/underthecherryblossomsfb

Historic Downtown with Modernism Museum:
>juliannescoastalcottage.com
>leefusionartglass.com
>modernismmuseum.org/collection

Jones Brothers Air and Seaplane Adventures:
>jonesairandsea.com

Lakeside Inn:
>lakeside-inn.com

Las Palmas Cuban Restaurant:
laspalmascubanrestaurant.com

Lawn Bowling Club:
mountdoralawnbowling.com

The Windsor Rose Restaurant and British Tea Room:
windsorrose-tearoom.com

Yacht Club:
mountdorayachtclub.com

Lighthouse at Grantham Point Park:
ci.mount-dora.fl.us/facilities/facility/details/Grantham-Point-8

Long & Scott Farm – Maze Adventures:
longandscottfarms.com

Maggie's Attic:
maggiesattic.us

Mount Dora Bicycle Festival:
mountdorabicyclefestival.com

Mount Dora Brewing and the Rocking Rabbit Brewery:
mountdorabrewing.com

Museum of History:
mountdorahistorymuseum.com

One Flight Up & The Secret Garden & Wayfinder:
facebook.com/OneFlightUp
secretgardenmtdora.com

Princess Theater:
mainstreetleasing.com/properties/76-130-w-5th-ave.html

Renningers Antique Center & Street of Shops and Flea & Farmer's Market:
renningers.net/index.php/main-locations/mount-dora/mount-dora-home

Seal of Mount Dora:
whattodoinmtdora.com/
ci.mount-dora.fl.us/27/Government

Segway of Central Florida:
segwayofcentralflorida.com

Sonnentag Theatre at the Icehouse:
icehousetheatre.com

Find out More About Mount Dora by Visiting These Websites:
whattodoinmtdora.com
visitmountdora.com